ISLAM
AND THE
TRANSFORMATION
OF CULTURE

ISLAM
AND THE
TRANSFORMATION
OF CULTURE

M. JAMIL HANIFI
Department of Anthropology,
Northern Illinois University, De Kalb

ASIA PUBLISHING HOUSE, INC.
New York

© 1970 Mohammed Jamil **Hanifi**

First Published 1974

ISBN 0.210. 40551.1

Library of Congress Catalog Card Number: 73-91139

PRINTED IN THE UNITED STATES OF AMERICA

For my son, Shah Mahmoud,
and all the Children of Islam

PREFACE

THE MUSLIM WORLD is undergoing disproportionate but rapid transformation. Virtually all of Muslim nation-states are now independent and self-governing. Islam, pervading so much of life as it does, has been the great force supporting tradition and the *status quo*. At the same time, ever increasing numbers of Muslims are articulating their preferences for things "modern" and "Western." Whatever degree of conflict between traditionalism and modernism develops in this interaction of desires, nowhere in the world has the metamorphosis of society forced such a dramatic rethinking of established values as in the contemporary Muslim World — particularly Turkey.

A steady trend toward secularization in traditional institutions is a feature of Muslim societies facing the impact of modern civilization. The Muslim peoples have different ethnic and cultural origins, geographic situations, historical background, and present-day conditions; the changes occurring among them differ in scope, intensity, and velocity. Still, one cannot avoid noting certain similarities in their experiences of socio-cultural change.

The disparity between the new and the old is perhaps to be found nowhere so clearly as in the lives of these peoples. Traditional cultural patterns are in the process of dissolution, and new forms have not yet become established. There are cleavages in almost every sector of life — in ideas, in institutions, between generations, and among classes and communities. Such a condition of flux is an unmistakable sign of internal changes in the value system of a society; and this change is unavoidably followed by some degree of secularization and a shift from a "prescriptive" to "principial" value orientation.

The process is universal throughout the Muslim World, but the attitude towards the problems created by it differs in every case. The acceptance of a secular orientation on religious, political, social, and cultural matters is far from universal. That such an outlook is warranted or ever relevant under the present conditions of flux is far from being generally recognized, let alone accepted.

The object of this work is to provide the reader with an analysis of Islam and Islamic Law and their evolution, along with their potentiality for "technicization," with particular reference to the Turkish transformation whose beginning goes back as far as the early part of the eighteenth century. A study of this transformation and the model proposed in Chapter IX may contribute to an understanding of contemporary conditions in many Muslim countries; but apart from this, it will be helpful to those who are interested in the comparative study of law, politics, and religious transformation in non-Western, Muslim societies.

The discussion is focused on the question of the relationship between religion and state, but the scope of the work is broader for two reasons: first, in order to present the context of processes affecting relations between state and religion, and second, because those relations have a wider connotation in the case of Islam than in that of Christianity. Thus, the process of secularization has been examined here as it has or can affect many aspects of society. This examination leads to the discussion of a doctrine of secularism that emerged as the basis of a policy of government and religion. The model of "technicization" proposed is in part based on this analysis.

The survey will deal largely with the development and changes in ideas and cultural values rather than with economic, demographic, or other material conditions of change although reference will be made to them when necessary. It should not, however, be taken primarily as a history of religious, scientific, political, educational, or legal ideas in Turkey. These have been described only insofar as they serve as indices of cultural change and the evolution of views, especially in the secularization of thought.

I am deeply grateful to many persons whom I cannot enumerate here. I owe special thanks to Roy Wagner for his suggestions and constructive criticism. I should like to thank Miss Denise Mazer for her invaluable help in typing the preliminary draft of this manuscript and for her suggestions regarding the editorial improvement of the text. Above all, I feel a particular debt of gratitude to my wife, without whose constant help and moral support this work would not have been completed.

CONTENTS

CHAPTER ONE

INTRODUCTION

IN RECENT YEARS there has developed an increasing recognition of the mutual dependence between changes in economic activity and organization and changes in social structure. Taken in its simplest form, this interrelationship has usually been expressed as a very general premise: economic development is only possible if the social structure of an underdeveloped system is developed so as to prove receptive to changes in conjunction with economic development plans, which invariably are designed after Western models. Hoselitz stated this idea when he concluded that if any successful development is to take place, the countries of Asia, Africa, and Latin America will have to adopt social institutions and social values resembling those of the West (1963:14-17).

Economic growth has everywhere occurred interwoven with political and social change. Lipset and Coleman have demonstrated the correlation between economic change and the transition from authoritarian to competitive secular politics in Asia, Africa, and Latin America. The same relation is found elsewhere including the Islamic societies such as Turkey, which has entered upon economic growth (Lipset 1951; Almond and Coleman 1960; Hagen 1962a; Hagen 1962b). The timing is such that it is clear that the economic growth does not occur first and cause the political-social change. Rather, the two are mutually dependent. Whatever the forces for change may be, they impinge on every aspect of human behavior. A theory of the transition to economic progress which does not simultaneously explain political change, or explains it merely as a consequence of the economic change, and the purely economic theories of barriers to cultural change which explain the absence of growth, all seem inadequate. The assumptions that the income of entire population is too low to make saving easy and capital investment possible; and that markets in low income countries are too small to induce investment are misleading. These and related theories which invariably pertain to Islamic societies are internally consistent but seem without great relevance to reality. Empirical study of low income Muslim societies demonstrates that the supposed conditions and requirements do not in fact exist or are not of great importance. Neither are the differences among Muslim nations with respect to economic development explained by differences in the degree of contact with the West. Cultural contact with the technical knowledge of the West is a requisite for growth, but forces quite independent of the degree of contact determine whether and how a society uses that knowledge.

Geertz (1960:105-106), regarding the Javanese Muslims reflects in a similar vein:

> The extent and excellence of a nation's resources, the size and skill of its labor force, the scope and complexity of its productive 'plant,' and the distribution and value of entrepreneural abilities among its population are only one element in the assessment of its capacity for economic growth; the institutional arrangements by means of which these various factors can be brought to bear on any particular economic goal is another.... It is for this reason that economic development in 'underdeveloped' areas implies much more than capital transfers, technical aid, and ideological exhortation: It demands a deep going transformation of the basic structure of society and, beyond

that, perhaps even in the underlying value-system in terms of which that structure operates.

The proper analogy of this position in the Muslim societies, then, turns out to be, not this or that motivational or institutional component, but reformation itself. What we need to discern is the "transformation of the basic structure of society" and its "underlying value-system," to use Geertz' language.

The aim of this dissertation is first to discern and discuss the main structural features of Turkey, an Islamic society. Particular reference will be made to the overwhelming characterization of the various structural components of this society by Islam. Secondly, it will be argued that the unity of polity and religion in pre-revolutionary Turkey was an acute impeding factor regarding technicization. Thirdly, it is the purpose of this dissertation to put forth a model for secularization (based on the experience of Turkey) for the Islamic states which would prove more conducive to a modernizing cultural transformation. A discussion of Islamic law will also be provided to illuminate and substantiate relevant points of consideration.

The main thesis of the model discussed in Chapter Nine is the divorcing of religion from politics and economic institutions in Islamic states. The consequence of such separations will result in releasing the frozen forces of innovation which in turn will bring about a structural realignment in the Muslim world. This would provide for effective implementation of designs and schemes for economic growth and modernization.

My aim is not to indulge in a discussion of the varieties of economic models, but simply to illustrate that Islam as a religion, as a state, and as the overriding theme in the structural arrangement of Islamic societies and in the life of its believers, is not receptive to progressive change, especially in the politico-economic sphere. Thus, if productive transformation and supplementary technicization is to be successful, significant alterations in the structure of Islamic societies, particularly in respect to Islamic law, and in conjunction with the features mentioned above, is imperative.

In the light of my theoretical interests and for the purpose of geographic specificity, emphasis will be placed on Turkey. Nevertheless, it is my conviction that the generalizations developed here can be applied to a wider range of Islamic societies without much qualification.

Chapter Two deals with the major characteristics of Islam, with particular reference to its overwhelming engulfment of everyday life and the nature of obstacles it has and can provide for the transformation of the Muslim societies. A discussion of technicization in Chapter Three will provide the theoretical framework of this dissertation. Chapter Four is a discussion of Islamic Law and its modern and traditional varieties. Emphasis will be placed on those features of *Sharia* which have proven most difficult to reconcile with modernizing processes. It has been argued that the Koran, as a legislative document, does not expressly provide solutions for the legal problems that face Muslim communities in their plight to uproot the stagnant level of their cultural settings. Consideration will be given in Chapter Five to the organization of Islam sociologically and historically.

It will be argued that political instability, which is here considered to be a major barrier to meaningful change, has been the hallmark of Muslim systems. Muslim systems have been and are characterized by tensions and balances that are hindrances to change. Nevertheless, the balance-tension level in Islamic systems has provided for lack of major integrative forces for its viability. Chapter Six is a critical discussion of reformist activities, with particular regard to legal transformation and secularization of the Muslim systems. Chapter Seven is concerned specifically with the problem of legal development and change in the Muslim world. The close link between Islam and law, it is pointed out, has threatened the legal flexibility that seems to be an important pre-requisite of a modern, techno-scientifically advanced society (Hoebel 1964). It will be pointed out how this traditional inflexibility was established in the modern Islamic world and how it is being circumvented. Chapter Eight provides for a discussion of secular education in Turkey and an examination of the extent to which secularization can be introduced through education and if done so, what problems are to be encountered. The argument is that educational institutions are at the heart of Islamic life everywhere and are thus a key area in which to study change. The shift from medieval to modern educational forms and orientations is of profound significance in the adaptation of Turkish Islam to the realities of modern life. It is pointed out that although secular education provides for a better foundation to modernize, however, it takes more than secular education to transform a Muslim system for it to harmonize its inner workings with modernization and progressive change. To be able to do so, a total secularization, a shift from prescriptive to principal values is argued for in Chapter IX. Once again Turkey provides the basis of the model proposed in this chapter.

Chapter X provides some conclusions and a discussion of the problems and prospects for the modernizing processes in the Muslim world. I have refrained from offering panaceas and piecemeal solutions to pressing problems. The model in Chapter Nine is only a tentative alternative, since it has proven to be relatively effective, at least in the case of Turkey. However, the limitations of the model are also pointed out in the hope that other relevant areas of problem and significance would be explored. On the other hand, it is my firm belief that at this juncture there is an acute need for a beginning. It is hoped that regardless of how much this beginning is limited, it is worth trying. It is only after experiencing one alternative that a system can later provide for others or at least appreciate, with a clear conscience, the one they have already chosen.

Although the references to Islam have been made in a general sense, the particular concern here is with the Sunni variety. When necessary and needed, specific similarities and/or dissimilarities between Sunni Islam and the Shi'a version will be noted.

SOME BASIC FEATURES OF ISLAM

CHAPTER TWO

SOME BASIC FEATURES OF ISLAM

THE FOCAL POINT of any traditional society and culture is religion. Many religions, Judaism, Christianity, and Islam; pagan, polytheistic, and monotheistic; local, tribal and universal, functioned at various times, and are operative at the present times as the principal foci of society in Muslim Asia and have provided for its rich historical legacy. For most of the past 1200 years, the region has been dominated by the last of the great monotheistic religions to emerge in the area—Islam.

Islam is today the religion of 95 per cent (Baer 1964 : 71) of the populations and therefore it is the focal point in Central and Southwest Asian society and culture. The remaining 5 per cent of the population constitute small vestigial pockets of Christians and Jews who occupy a special status within the Islamic community. To understand the traditional Islamic society in this region and its adjustment to the Western ideas of progress and development, it is therefore essential to focus upon the Islamic religion. Processes of the alleged adjustment have been costly. It has produced in the Islamic society "a psychological unsettlement, the effects of which

were reinforced successively by the derangement of their old social
and economic structure and the intrusion of Western thought"
(Gibb 1955: 132). For this reason, the problem of Islamic adaptation to the modern world is one of the major themes of this dissertation, with particular emphasis on Muslim values, institutions,
and Islamic Law. At this point my purpose is not a detailed
analysis of Islam but merely to emphasize the fact that Islam is the
single most consistent and pervasive socio-cultural force in the
regions inhabited by a substantial Muslim population.

"Islam" literally means submission and in the socio-religious
context it means submission to the will of God (Kerr 1966: 58),
called Allah in Arabic. A Muslim is one who has submitted to
Allah and who acknowledges Mohammed as the messenger of God.
In his profession of faith, repeated in five daily prayers, the
Muslim proclaims, "there is no God but Allah, and Mohammed
is his messenger."   ·

Unlike modern Western society, in which religion is so often
reserved for Sunday and such special occasions as marriage and
death, traditional Islam is all-embracing. All social relations are
defined, determined, and sanctioned by religion. Functional differentiations along political, economic, social and religious lines,
characteristic of the Muslim world, do not exist. Instead, there is a
unity between religion and society. There is no division between
the temporal and religious, between the secular and sacred (Smith
1964). An Islamic spirit permeates the entire area and all aspects
of life—private, political, social, economic, and religious (Lerner
1964: 404).

Symbolic of the role that Islam plays in the lives of Muslims is
the practice, immediately after a child is born, "to repeat the
words of the call to prayer (*adhan*) into the child's right ear and
into his left ear, so as to accustom him to Muslim confessions of
faith" (Gaudefray-Demonbynes 1954 : 1959). As the traditional
Muslim child grows up, his enculturation, socialization, and education continually stress religion. Moreover, "the set phrases of
polite speech and the social gestures which are all so many affirma-
tions of Islamic values, the daily conversations punctuated by
eulogies of, and invocations to the Prophet illustrate the tight
control religion exercises over daily life" (Bourdieau 1962: 107).

The truth is that in Muslim society all social conventions are impregnated with religion. Even pre-Islamic customs and traditions that may be of pagan origin are given religious sanctions. Perhaps the most noteworthy of this is the Kaaba, the meteorite black stone located in Mecca which has assumed a central position in the Islamic pilgrimage ritual even though it was revered by local pre-Islamic pagan tribes from pre-historic times. According to Muslim tradition, the Kaaba was originally built by Adam as the house of God and was rebuilt by Abraham with Ismael's help after it was destroyed by the flood (Watt 1964 : 187). There are many other illustrations of Islamic doctrine and ritual accommodating themselves to local traditions. For example, the Islamic injunction against images did not succeed in Iran where the pre-Muslim heritage of painting persisted. In various parts of the Muslim world, local customs have been given religious sanctions, and have become as hallowed as the overall Islamic tradition (Bacon 1966).

To the particular Muslim concerned, his unique folk customs are considered no less Muslim and sacred than those formally prescribed by the universal tradition (Geertz 1968). Thus, when we speak of traditional Islam we must recognize, that two strains are involved, the universal and local (pre-Islamic).

The incorporation of local customs within the Islamic framework took place out of necessity rather than by design. Islam's sacred code of law, the Sharia (straight path, based essentially on the Koran and the Hadith, the tradition of the Prophet) did not provide specific legal guidance for every circumstance and situation. In theory, the Sharia was all-embracing but it had to be supplemented by local traditions and new laws to deal with new issues.

Despite local deviations, it is noteworthy that all traditional Muslims are guided by Islamic law and traditions. It is only a limited cultural pluralism that exists within and under the protection of the unity of Islam (von Gruenbaum 1955: 24). All Muslims form part of a universal order, known as the Dar-al-Islam or House of Submission, which stands opposed to the Dar-al-Harb or House of War, and constitutes the community of believers, the Ummah.

The existence of sects and divisions within Islam, while of great importance from the standpoint of regional diversities in social and cultural patterns, does not distract from the significant cultural homogeneity with which religion endows Islamic societies. In cases where there is a presence of other religious themes, such as in Israel, and Lebanon, but a substantial Muslim population, this homogeneity does not significantly diminish. As a result of the local deviations, it is clear that Islam does not constitute a mono-lithic order. One can safely talk of an Islamic ethos in the same way that one refers to a Christian-Judaic ethos.

The actual unity of Islam was, in fact, disrupted very early in its history by the conflict over the succession of the Caliph from the Arabic word Khalifa (meaning successor) shortly after the death of Mohammed. This issue led to the schism out of which emerged the great division within Islam, the Sunni (followers of the tradi-tion) and the Shi'a (followers of Ali). It also set a precedent for further divisions in later generations (Brockelman 1960).

The great majority of all Muslims are Sunni although the Shias constitute an important cultural and political factor in the Islamic world. There are 40-50 million Shias in the world, about 10-15 per cent of the Islamic community (Baer 1964: 103). The differences between Sunnis and Shias are not primarily theological. Shiaism originated as an Arab political movement to restore the house of Ali to the Caliphate and took on many aspects of a lower class revolt against the ruling Sunni hierarchy (Coulson 1964: 103). For many years Shi'aism continued to share the Sunni doctrine and creed and it was only much later that unique doctrine in law and theology evolved. However, these unique features are overridden by the overwhelming similarity between the two sects in regard to their consistent and restrained pre-occupation with the maintenance of the status quo. The most important consequence of the Sunni-Shi'a schism lies in its potential as a potent divisive force in the Islamic world, not in matters of the creed as it is practiced, but in conjunction with the articulation and comprehension of the Islamic tradition, particularly in regard to the question of succes-sion to Mohammed.

The concept of Dar-al-Islam established the theoretical frame-work for a unified Muslim world, just as the concept of "the church" a unified Christendom. With some exceptions among

lesser sects, Islam has no centralized authority, neither in the
religious nor in the temporal sense. There is no overall ecclesiasti-
cal clergy and in theory Islam dispenses almost completely with
an organized religious hierarchy. In practice, a religious "elite"
known as the Ulema (learned men of the law) emerge, wielding
considerable authority. And it is the Ulema who have provided
the most impenetrable obstacle to change, development and
progress. By the same token, if meaningful change is to be effectively implemented, the eradication or at least the weakening of the
base of support of the Ulema is imperative. The members of this
group are the formal interpreters of the Koranic Law and the
chief apostles of the status quo. In most Islamic societies with
which this writer is familiar, social-civil legislation passed by the
"parliaments" and other law-making agencies must be screened
by the so-called "Ministry(s) of Justice" who are invariably staffed
by the Ulema, for checking possible deviations from the Sharia.
This quite obviously accounts, to a large extent, for the lack of
progressive civil legislation conducive and adaptive to the presence
(or the potential presence) of internal and/or external pressures
for transformation. The threat, or the possibility of the real exercise of such veto powers, is enough to thwart reform movements,
progressive thought, and innovations, in the legislative sphere and
in the socio-cultural plane at large.

"All innovation is the work of the devil" (Levy 1958 : 205).
These alleged words of the founder prophet of Islam, Mohammed,
do not merely reflect the innate conservatism and the deep-
seated attachment to tradition that were so strong among the
Arab peoples who formed the first adherents to the faith. They
also express a principle that became a fundamental axiom of
religious belief in Islamic communities everywhere, namely, the
code of conduct represented by the religious law, or Sharia, was
fixed and final in its terms and that any modification would necessarily be a deviation from one legitimate and valid standard.

Among Muslim peoples, therefore, it is what we may call the
traditional or classical Islamic concept and its role in society that
constitutes a most formidable obstacle to progress and development. Western jurisprudence has provided a number of different
answers to questions about the law, finding its sources in the orders

of political superiors, in the confines of the judiciary, in the internal processes of a changing society, or in the very nature of the universe itself. For Islam, however, this same question admits of only one answer, which the religious faith itself supplies, law is the command of Allah, and the acknowledged functions of Muslim jurisprudence from the beginning was simply to discern the terms of that command. Consensus is the function of the Muslim community. Indeed the Sharia, as it emanates from the Koran, has as its fundamental purpose to maintain and perpetuate this state of consensus (Watt 1961; Coulson 1964).

The religious code of conduct thus established was an all-embracing one, in which many aspects of human relationships were regulated in meticulous detail. Furthermore, the law, having once achieved perfection of expression, was in principle static and immutable. Therefore, the religious law was to float above Muslim society as a disembodied soul, representing the eternally valid ideal toward which society must aspire.

In classical Islamic theory, therefore, law does not grow out of or develop along with an evolving society, as is the case with Western systems, but is imposed from above. In the Islamic concept, human thought unassisted cannot discern the values and standards of conduct; such knowledge can be attained only through divine revelation, and acts are good or evil exclusively because Allah has attributed this quality to them. Law therefore precedes and is not preceded by society; it controls and is not controlled by society. Although in Western systems the law is molded by society, in Islam exactly the opposite is true (Ward and Rustow 1964). The religious law provides the comprehensive, divinely ordained, and eternally valid master plan to which the structure of state and society must ideally conform. The clash between the dictates of the rigid and static Islamic law and the values that it embodies and any impetus for change, development and progress that a system may experience poses for Islam a fundamental problem of principle. This will be discussed in detail later on.

Thus Islam represents a vital contemporary social force in the Islamic countries, most obviously because most of the population shares its theological belief systems. The most significant implication is that the society is resistant to change and cannot go counter to sanctified traditions. As a result, many political and intellectual leaders in regions dominated by Islam share the dilemma of reconciling, in vain, economic and general socio-cultural reform with the traditional well-grounded principles of Islam. There are, however, instances where religion (Islam) has provided a rather superficial support for modernization (Iran and Turkey). But such accommodation has been temporary since they have been arranged in a "shotgun" framework without much consideration to the intrinsic incompatibility of Muslim ideology that runs counter to the maintenance and elaboration of techno-scientific thought—the foundation of modern Western technological developments (Jacobs 1967; Berkes 1967).

Nor is the influence of Islam limited to the faithful. It also has a strong national appeal, though for different reasons, for most of the emancipated Westernized 20 per cent of the population (Hourani 1947), having been raised in an Islamic cultural milieu, cannot and often do not desire to be cut off fully from the Islamic community with which they identify, and of which they feel themselves a part. This feeling was and is reinforced by the discriminatory attitudes of the Westerners as colonists, particularly in Central and Southwest Asia. Europeans have not welcomed close associations with any "native," even the Western educated Muslims who were most influenced by the West (Berger 1962: Chapters Nine and Ten). Thus, the elite was alienated from the West and today the great majority identify with Islam as part of their "nationalist" creed.

To be sure, economic underdevelopment and cultural staticism is not restricted to the Islamic world. It is perhaps more pronounced here than elsewhere, but it is certainly not unique. A drastic economic imbalance, so predominant in Islamic societies, is itself a symptom of something deeper. The fact has often been stressed that economic problems cannot be divorced from the total content of the culture. The crisis brought about by the acute lack of development is seriously aggravated, if not induced, by underlying Islamic cultural conditions. The recent history of the whole of Asia bears this out (Hudson 1952). But whereas the rest of Asia has been suffering from social and cultural decline for a few generations, the Islamic world has been the victim of the same malady for centuries.

Islam was destined from the very beginning to become a dominant feature of society, far more so than any other major religion. For it was Mohammed's conviction that his mission included the task of founding a community which should be a state as well as a religion (Abbot 1968). Numerous tenets of Islam reflect the intimate blending of the spiritual and the temporal (Jeffery 1942:383). But while spiritual values often prove to be enduring, temporal policies, as the name implies, presently become outdated. By now, Islam as a spiritual experience has stood the test of time for some thirteen centuries. But it is the state religion in most countries within the Islamic world. To the extent to which Islam is a state as much as a religion, the effect of the system on progressive development and remedial change has been negative for a long time.

It is neither feasible nor necessary to trace here in detail the inhibitive aspects of traditional Islam in the cultural life of its community throughout the centuries. The long term results in general have proved harmful in precisely those fields that affect the vitality of the social system as a whole. Thus, the Muslim laws of succession and the institutions of the Waqf, or pious foundations, have jointly contributed to the progressive fragmentation of landholdings and the critical inequality of land ownership (Himadeh 1951:272). Education in a theocratic state is of necessity slanted, limited, and reactionary. This is so because the primary function of the educational agencies becomes to sustain the state (*status quo*) and not the well-being of the system at large. Further, an educational process that has as its prime purpose to conserve rather than to change can neither provide the stimulus nor the operational facility for progressive dynamism. Under such conditions social practices remain stagnant, innovation and entrepreneurship are inhibited. Thus, development and progress are choked. The cases of such theocratic states such as Afghanistan, Saudi Arabia, Iran, Yemen, and other Muslim theocracies provides substantive illustrations to this effect.

The pervasive weakness of Islamic society, therefore, is due in large measure to the dominant temporal features of the underlying system. The obvious answer to the problem would be a resolute separation of religion and state (as elaborated in Chapter V). This is by no means a novel solution. It is implicit, for instance, in the statement of a distinguished Syrian educator and statesman, Costik Zuryak, who has written as follows (1949 : 127):

When, however, it (Islam) became reduced to a set of doctrines to be taken on credence, and a code of laws and morals to be applied rigidly and blindly it turned out to be, as other religions in the same state, a burden rather than an inspiration, a paralyzing shackle instead of a liberating force, the letter that killeth all real endeavor and progress.

A courageous Egyptian Muslim, Khalid Mohammed Khalid, refers to the same conditions in terms of witchcraft rather than religion (Khalid 1953). Yet the logical step of divorcing state from religion has been taken by only one of the Muslim countries, namely, Turkey. And it is surely no mere coincidence that Turkey today is perhaps the most progressive and dynamic Muslim country. But the rest of the Islamic community has yet to reverse its downward trend.

It follows at any rate that Islam is the dominant structural feature in Muslim societies. The name implies submission to divine authority, and the entire history of the Islamic community points to the system as an overriding cultural factor and the major, and at times, the only, barrier to progressive change. Accordingly, different conditions may be looked for where the influence of Islam is either negligible or has been measurably reduced. Such indeed is the case, for example, in three states in the predominantly Muslim Southwest Asia. Israel has but a small Muslim minority, hence her socio-economic, and political status is markedly different from that of her neighbors. Lebanon is half Christian, with a consequent reduction in the influence and strength of Islam and in the social unbalance from which Syria, Afghanistan, Pakistan, Iran, Iraq, or a Saudi Arabia is suffering. And while Turkey is overwhelmingly Muslim, her progressive career in recent years dates back exactly to the time when religion was removed officially from the socio-political sphere. But if this could happen in Muslim Turkey, why have not the other Muslim states followed suit?

The question is a logical one. The answer is bound up with the further features of the various cultural themes and, more importantly, the degree of penetration of Islam in the incipient non-Islamic cultural plane, as demonstrated by Geertz in his comparison of Islam in Morocco and in Indonesia (1968), and other differences within the Islamic community that contribute to the uniqunesses in national group personalities, that are roughly reflected in the many Islamic states. To put it differently, Pakistan, the Arab states, and Afghanistan, for example, have not followed the example of Turkey, at least not so far, because the circumstances have not been the same in each instance. This is, of course, a plain fact. But it is scarcely valid to account for that fact with the invariable cliche that Turkey has had its Mustafa Kamal Ataturk whereas the other Muslim states have not. The personal equation is important but will not bear much probing in this context. A man may hope to change the course of a national culture only when the component culture is made ready or is prepared for the process. Otherwise, the change will prove superficial and short-lived at best. Much that is not apparent on the surface went into the making of modern Turkey. And since that formative background has led to results which seem to distinguish Turkey from other Muslim cultural spheres (perhaps with the exception of Muslim groupings in Soviet Central Asia), the factor in question would be essentially the reorganization of Islam, as we shall see later on.

TECHNICIZATION: A THEORETICAL
FRAMEWORK

CHAPTER THREE

TECHNICIZATION:
A THEORETICAL FRAMEWORK

CULTURAL ANALYSIS HAS long been preoccupied with those features of traditional cultures which affect the direction and content of change and the receptivity of a society to innovation. In spite of the very considerable literature concerned with cultural change, there have been few efforts to examine different types of traditional systems with respect to problems posed for cultural "modernization." Most theories on cultural change have not addressed themselves to the basic refinement and clarification of the concepts they have utilized. Indeed, many anthropologists have failed to explicitly articulate the phenomenon that is to be changed or changing. The basic concern has been with describing the progress of change and the mechanisms or cultural features that generate change. Indeed, many students of change have refused to address themselves to the direction and content of the process involved in cultural transformation. Only recently there have been attempts made to relegate the general category "cultural change" for a more precise concept such as "modernization," "Westernization," "development," etc. A review of some of the approaches will place some light on some of the contemporary approaches in the study of cultural change and the difficulties they pose in attempting to organize a unified synthesis of the process of cultural dynamics (its direction and content).

Barnett (1953) has put forth a theory that makes it necessary to postulate some new factors to account for changes in approved norms. Such changes are commonly thought of as the adoption by individuals of "new ways," and explained in terms of learning theory. Thus Barnett in his book, *Innovation*, discusses all the circumstances that may favor or discourage innovation in any kind of society. He reminds us that innovation of one kind or another is going on all the time, and for him no innovation, be it only a new way of making a gesture, is too small to be included in his generalizations. He is concerned with innovations that are imitated and so become standardized as accepted forms of behavior, but, though he recognizes that innovations are encouraged in some fields and discouraged in others, he does not treat this as a significant factor for the study of cultural change. Thus, he remarks that in American culture, changes in technology are expected but not changes in religion, in political structure, or in family organization; in other words, mechanical inventions are encouraged but social deviation is not. This statement in fact puts in a nutshell what seems to be the crucial problem of cultural change among Muslim societies in general and in the case of Turkey (discussed later on). For Muslims, it is true, there is no need to make mechanical inventions (they can borrow them), but the problem of adjusting themselves to the use of such inventions arises precisely out of the resistance that is built in the conservative structure of Islamic society.

Barnett might question this statement, since he quotes the Samoans as a society in which everyone is expected to be different from everyone else not only in inventing songs and dance steps and designs to stamp on cloth, but in "religion and political organization." Nevertheless, the Samoans recognize rules of rank and precedence, and indeed they employ specialist officials to recite the order of precedence among the aristocrats of each district; and care enough about these rules to have secured a special position for the aristocrats in the constitution given to them by the United States. No social order would be possible without some generally accepted picture of the roles appropriate to the relationships in which people find themselves, and some confidence that these roles would be appropriately performed. This confidence is everywhere maintained by constant social pressures tending to reward conformity and penalize deviation. What is interesting in the study of cultural change is precisely the question of what kind of counterpressure (such as an ideology that can at least tolerate deviation, if not encourage it openly) makes non-conformity worthwhile, and this is an aspect of the subject that I feel has practical significance for the transformation of traditional Muslim orders.

Others have suggested an increase in the "scale" of the society which facilitates progressive change and "economic development" (Wilson and Wilson 1945). Thus, the size of a society has a direct relation to technological receptivity. By the scale of a society it is meant that the "number of people in relation and the intensity of those relations....In comparing the scale of societies, therefore, we compare the relative size of groups with relations of similar intensity" (Wilson and Wilson 1945: 25).

The Wilsons argue that change ("economic growth") occurs when we have individuals whose background includes acquaintance with more than one community. The implication of this position is that if the world of an individual includes only a single village (at least in central Africa which provides the raw data for this scheme), the range of facts he has observed is probably so limited that he will hardly have that understanding of the diversity of causes and effects in the world which is a prerequisite to innovation.

Obviously, economic growth often occurs in one region of a country and only later spreads to the entire nation—as is happening in many developing countries. Hence a fullfledged sense of nationhood is not an absolutely necessary condition. But cultural progress is hardly possible until there has been some expansion of the sense of local unity beyond the local community. But we must be aware of the fact that such an expansion would be meaningless if conditions beyond the local community were not uniformly better than what the community is already under—materially and ideologically. Further, expansion of the scale of a society can hardly be taken as a starting point in the analysis of social change except with the admission that one is breaking into the middle of a dynamic process without attempting to probe its origins. Also, expansion does not occur either by accident or by some inevitable force which can be attributed to nature or to "the nature of things." Something, internal or external, generates it.

Some authors such as McClelland (1961) argue that such an increase could be realized by a parallel increase in personality characteristics termed need achievement. McClelland is concerned with interactions among social organization, individual behavior, and economic development. "In its most general terms," he says, "the hypothesis states that a society with a generally high level of n-achievement will produce energetic entrepreneurs who, in turn, will produce more rapid economic development" (1961: 205). His book *The Achieving Society* tries "to isolate certain psychological factors and to demonstrate rigorously by quantitative scientific methods that these factors are generally important in economic development" (1961: ix). He admits that "psychologist has been of little help to date" in the understanding of economic development, but he feels that recent improvements in techniques for measuring motivation permit the application of psychology to "a problem of real interest to economists and sociologist" (1961: 18-19). His work in this framework in regard to Turkey is discussed in a later chapter.

One must admit that McClelland's work is bold, imaginative, and entertaining. But it is hard to see what there is about his loosely related series of psychological experiments and statistical tests that makes his methodology more "rigorously empirical" than the cautious work of the econometricians who like to have a tight, logically consistent theoretical model, mathematically expressed, to begin with.

If McClelland is telling us that societies conducive to the generation of effective entrepreneurship are likely to have more rapid development than societies that are not, he is not adding much to our knowledge. To make a real contribution, he must be able to identify n-achievement clearly as an independent variable, measure it in uniform manner permitting interspatial and intertemporal comparisons, show precisely that there is a stronger link between this variable and entrepreneurship than there is between entrepreneurship and other variables, and tell us how to *create* or *direct* n-achievement in operational terms. His work, stimulating as it is, falls far short of meeting these criteria.

Robert Levine, in comparing the Hausa, the Ibo, and the Yoruba indulges in the same type of analysis, and finds the Hausa of Nigeria to have a lesser degree of n-achievement. It just happens that the Hausa are Muslims and Levine's subscription to what McClelland had to say about the Turks, who are also Muslims, are confirmed. There are, however, some points in Levine's treatment which McClelland does not consider. "The only point at which this hypothetical framework departs from that of McClelland is in the first variable (status mobility), which is social structural rather than part of a system of religious belief" (Levine 1966: 18-19). Levine contends that it is not "plausible" to "assume that parental values can be represented by the consensus surrounding a well-established, legitimated, status mobility system" (1966: 19). It is hypothesized that "participation in an adult society in which major social rewards are given to those who do best on their own in competition with a standard of excellence" (Levine 1966: 19). Thus, the values subscribed to and operationalized by the adult members are just as important as the kind of molded individual who becomes a consequence of such value subscriptions. Here again, one is not clear as to what is the "type" of personality that is conducive to innovation and more importantly what is the direction and content of change to which a possible innovative type would ultimately contribute. In addition, Levine's conclusions regarding the Muslim Hausa suffer from an imbalanced treatment. His data is quite substantive for his other two groups, while he tells us little about the Hausa. More seriously, it is my reading that Levine is following a rather futile course. It is ironic that neither of the authors discussed above tell anything in regard to what the ends of innovation ought to be. Innovation for the sake of innovation seems to be textbook science with no relevance to the outside immediate needs of human affairs on the ground.

It is interesting that most purposive models of change have been articulated by sociologists, not anthropologists. Moore (1965) and Levy (1966) come closest to setting forth not only the socio-cultural process that leads to meaningful change, but they also put forth explicitly what the end (quantifiable) consequence of such process should (will) be. Further, students of development such as Anderson and Bowen (1965) are quite clear as to the particular role a specific process such as education should and must play in the process of progressive cultural transformation. Few anthropologists including the ones cited here will boldly state that education is not only a vehicle of change but it should above all serve as the "stimulator and agent for change" (Anderson and Bowen 1963).

The sociologist's approach, nevertheless has been one of providing recipes for change. This is quite obvious in the structural approach put forth by Eisensdadt (1966), whereby an overall blueprint for an "idealized" structural arrangement is provided. Three main phases are differentiated: the pre-modernization, the process to become modernized (to be able to maintain technology, not necessarily the ability to create it), and lastly to stabilize and the maintaining of mechanism in the system for modernization. Thus the concern is with building institutional arrangements paralleling those of the Western systems with little regard or understanding of what specific ingredients are required not only to create technology but also to maintain it.

Wilbert Moore equates modernization with *industry* which he defines as "the fabrication of raw materials into intermediate components or finished products by primarily mechanical means dependent on inanimate sources of power" (1965: 4). Moore argues for a particular institutional arrangement that will be relevant to the "factory system." Further it is argued that a factory system will lead to industrialization and economic development which will in turn result in "structural changes." This is fine but what are the *specific* factors, those human-cultural factors that provide not only the foundation but also the overall framework and significant goals for such processes. None of the authors address themselves to such fundamental questions. Levy (1966) comes closest to providing an ideological "milieu" for such an industrializing, mechanically articulated process of transformation.

I have therefore refrained from paraphrasing the variety of definitions offered for "modernization." I believe it is sound and more profitable to define the means for techno-scientific change along with the intricate and detailed structural-ideological variables that enter in the process of purposive transformation.

In the light of the divergent views discussed above, the student of cultural change is ready to agree with Gabriel Almond that in this field, "the magnitude of the formal and empirical knowledge required...staggers the imagination and lames the will" (Almond 1960). In recent studies on the Muslim world, the complex character of the developmental process is duly acknowledged (Lerner 1964; Berkes 1964; and others). Nevertheless, considerable divergence of views are expressed with regard to the most effective conceptual framework to adopt in order to understand this process. There is agreement that the process of developmental change involves a progressive substitution of new modes of perception to replace those modes associated with traditionalism. However, apart from stating the obvious or spinning a web of tautologies, the tendency is to stay fairly close to the conceptual framework based upon the Weberian traditional-rational dichotomy.

Since the traditional and rational modes of perception and behavior coexist in even the most developed societies, "modernity" cannot involve the total substitution of rationality for traditionalism. Of course the mixture of the two, with the predominance of traditionalism characterize the Muslim systems. Instead, the achievement of a state of modernity must involve passing some critical point in the developmental process beyond which the rational mode of perception and behavior tends to dominate. Before this critical point has been reached, society is torn by the struggle between rationality and traditionalism, with each trying to define the scope of the other. As Lerner has noted in regard to Turkey and Iran, this is a time of tension, "village versus town, land versus cash, illiteracy versus enlightenment, resignation versus ambition, piety versus excitement" (1964). This tension, in turn, reflects the central dimension of the developmental process, namely, changing the "contents of man's minds." The process of change calls for considerably more than punctilious adherence to a recipe of two cups economic planning, one cup administrative reform, three teaspoons of land reform, and a dash of violence. What is called for is a fundamental intellectual reorientation, a shift from prescriptive to principial (see Chapter Nine) I shall call "ideational transformation." The term "ideational" is deliberately used in lieu of ideology for the following reasons: (i) the word "ideation" refers to the formation of ideas about things not present to the senses, a point I wish to emphasize; (ii) it does not carry the same value connotations as the term ideology; and (iii) it emphasizes perception more than a disposition to act. In brief, ideational transformation suggests the adoption of a totally new intellectual constructions, which will provide a unified solution to socio-cultural problems. Ideational transformation is a necessary precondition for development; it is not simply a final effect.

Ideational transformation in a Muslim (and of course in other traditional non-modern) society is always fractional, intermittent, and discontinuous. Those having made this transformation, at least in part such as in Turkey, constitute the modernizing elite. Their efforts to engender mass ideational transformation are impeded by a vast array of psychological, institutional, and structural obstacles (McClelland 1961). Moreover, the tendency on the part of the tradition-bound masses to interpret new ideas in terms of their own traditional framework, coupled with the efficaciousness of cloaking new ideas in traditional garb, makes it difficult, if not impossible, to gauge adequately the degree to which a society as a whole has actually made such an ideational transformation. As a result, a developing society, at any particular point in time, tends to give reflection to this intellectual dualism in the form of an unstable synthesis of both traditional and "modern" modes of perception. The progressive restatement of this synthesis over time to accommodate historical permutations suggests that the developmental process may be fruitfully perceived by analyzing the dialectical interaction of these two antipodal ideational orientations within a developing society. My purpose here is to examine this possibility in regard to Turkey in particular and other Islamic settings in general.

The style of thought and mode of behavior associated with Islamic traditionalism will serve as a convenient point of departure. The

ecological nature of Muslim societies may take much of its character
from geographical and climatological conditions, but the intellectual
foundations of the traditional culture in Muslim milieus derive directly from Islam, as will be observed in the following chapters, and as
alluded to in the preceding chapters. Any attempt to "diagnose
the situation" within Muslim societies without taking into account
the ubiquitous influence of Islam would produce only sterile and
distorted images of socio-cultural reality. Reflective of such distor-
tions are the works of Levine (1966), McClelland (1961), and
Moore (1965).

From the seventh to the tenth century, Islam was a most dynamic
force. A number of explanations have been put forth to account for
the subsequent stagnation of the Islamic world. Some have suggested that it was because of the havoc wrought by Mongol swords
(Rahman 1966), and few would question the fact that where the
Mongols did penetrate, the veneer of "civilization" was erased;
but the Mongols did not reach Egypt, Turkey, or Spain. Others
have underscored the venality of many Muslim leaders (Berkes
1964), but Islamic politicians hold no monopoly of these traits.
The truth of the matter is that the seed of intellectual stagnation
was nurtured by Islam itself, and subsequently spread to enfetter
the whole of society, and that seed was sown over two centuries
before Hulagu even reached the gates of Baghdad.

The nature of Islam led its followers to ask the wrong questions.
Preoccupation with legal matters and Islamic jurisprudence (*fiqh*),
as well as Koranic exegesis (*tafsir*), promoted an intellectual style
that tended to designate man as a being at once creative and
capable of doing. Only Allah and the Word is emphasized. This
orientation is to be compared to the Western tradition where, from
the seventeenth century at least, man takes on a hyperbolic pre-
ception of his own ability.

In the Islamic world, the law was "the epitome of Islamic
thought, the most typical manifestation of the Islamic way of life,
the core and kernel of Islam itself" (Schacht 1964: 1). Therefore,
when the "gate of independent interpretation" (*ijtihad*) was closed
in the tenth century in the field of Islamic jurisprudence and the
restrictive doctrine of imitation (*taqlid*) adopted for all Sunni
Muslims, the formative period of Islamic tradition was at an end.

As Philip Hitti has noted, the effect of this was that in theology and law, in science and philosophy, in literature and the humanities, Islam is today virtually what it was nine centuries ago (1962).

Particularly important in establishing the nature of contemporary Islamic tradition was the victory of the Ash'arite philosophy over that of the Mu'tazalite in the eleventh century. The latter's doctrine of free will was driven from the intellectual market place and fatalism and rigid predestinarianism raised to the level of orthodoxy. The ontological position of the Ash'arite is that relationships have no real existence, that causality is mere chimera, and that reality is but the product of constant, ever-repeated creations. Even time is nothing but "a succession of untouching moments." Their creed is, "without enquiring how and without making comparisons." With causality denied and the laws of nature mere appearances, the epistomological basis of orthodox (Sunni) Islam is exactly contrary to that suggested by scientific methodology. The road to knowledge is through revelation and/or the ecstatic experience of Sufi mysticism, not empiricism.

Inasmuch as my basic concern is with Sunni Islam, it must be pointed out that in Iran, where Shi'aism displaced Sunni'ism as the dominant creed in 1502, the intellectual preconditions of change fared no better.

Even though Shi'aism is predicated upon a structure of Mu'tazalite rationalism, the Shi'a doctrine of instruction (talim) has circumscribed the role of reason no less effectively than Ash'arite scholasticism by subordinating free inquiry to the limitations set by the authoritative pronouncements of an infallible Hidden Imam, with only conservatively oriented mujtahid empowered to give exegetical interpretation to Shi'ite dogma, pending the appearance of the now occulted Imam.

Thus, whether Sunni or Shi'a, Islamic traditionalism is, intellectually, uncritical and marked by fatalism (kismat) and predestinarianism. For the bulk of the Muslim society, the immediacy of Allah's will is a condition of life. Man is not master of his own fate—that is to be determined by Allah's inscrutable will.

Commenting on eighteenth century Turkey, Gibb and Bowen note in this connection, "The one unpardonable blasphemy was to complain of misfortune; for this was to imply that an event might occur otherwise than by the will of God, or else that the will of God was unjust. The correct response was an immovable calm and a reference to *Kismat* or *Taqdir*" (Gibb and Bowen 1955). That which by Islamic dogma or custom (*adat*) has been established is to be maintained; that which is innovation (*bida*) is to be eschewed.

Since "modernization" has been used in a rather misleading way in anthropological literature (as discussed earlier in this chapter) I shall not use the concept here. Obviously, the varied usages have their advantages and disadvantages. I am not convinced that the "recipe" approach to change is of particular advantage. To propose structural features of modernization as Eisendadt (1966: 2-19) does, imposes on one the rather impossible task of isolating the specific features required for a "modernized" level. On the other hand, the realization of these features will quite likely (when and if possible) facilitate the articulation of an ideation. But one must keep in mind that to realize such specific features, one needs a cultural context, direction, and above all, an ideation which will not only enhance the process through which these structural features will be built and give meaning and concreteness to the final structural form. Granted, we need the restructuring of systems before those systems become "modernized." But this reorganization will be meaningless in a cultural void and in the absence of an ideational orientation. It is this focus and ideation to which I shall concern myself, and which will provide the theoretical framework of this thesis and the model proposed in Chapter Nine.

In antipodal relationship to Islamic traditionalism is that ideational orientation which will be defined as "technicism" in this study. The term is not synonymous with rationalism, although the technicist would profess to being "rational." Neither is it the same as scientism, for science has gone far beyond the simple mechanistic determinism that still characterizes technicism. It is instead an intellectual orientation that rejects all that is spontaneous, contingent, anomic, irrational, unreflective, and idiosyncratic. Lasswell and Kaplan (1950) move close to the meaning of technicism in their differentiations of "techniques" from "technics," with the technicalization of society a consequence of the dissemination of the "scientific-explanatory and the engineering-manipulative perspective into every realm of culture.'' The technicalization of society thus flows from a prior adherence to the intellectual orientation of technicism.

The term "technicism" has been selected for a further reason. The Weberian traditional-rational dichotomy implies that rationalism is not a component of traditionalism, an interpretation that even Weber never intended. Both Islamic traditionalism and technicism are belief systems. Each is postulated on an axiom of faith. But what the Muslim interprets as the product of Allah's inscrutable will, technicism identifies as a reflection of man's superstition, or his contemporary state of ignorance. To the technicist, inherent in any problem is its solution. It is only a matter of ferreting out that solution by proper adherence to the canons of technicist methodology.

The ontology of technicism is a rationally ordered universe in mechanistic harmony, and subject to strict laws of causality. The universe is ethically neutral, or at least coincides with man as a moral being. The vicissitudes of history are a product of man's evolving perception of the universe, rather than Allah's arbitrary intervention. The theodicy of the technicist is a temporary condition, with history recording man's progressive liberation from the pitfalls of his own ignorance.

The epistemological basis of technicism is empiricism; there is no room in the realm of technicism for Aristotle's "weighty testimony of the poets.'' By its very nature, technicism is iconoclastic, assiduously striking down "truths" not verified by its own logic of proof. Propositions of reality based upon revelation, intuition, or ecstatic experience are rejected out of hand. Only those propositions subject to pragmatic verification are legitimate. Thus, technicism is: a technique of thinking and an epistemology, which has elevated the criteria of everyday experience to the level of "academic discussion.''

Within the framework of technicism, both time and measurable entities, terms of quantification, in fact, constitute the very lexicon of the technicist. One might even say that to the technicist, the universe is a statistical universe. To measure is to master, with all human and physical relationships understandable, and frequently manipulatable through variation of quantity.

Unlike Islamic traditionalism, technicism focuses its attention on relationships between concrete aspects of empirical reality. Thought is rational, in fact, when and only when it "reveals intelligent insight into the interrelations of events in a given situation" (Manheim 1940: 53). This restriction to the nature of rational thought does not preclude, of course, its use in traditional societies. Such societies do, in fact, "rationalize" facets of their socio-cultural life, and such rationalization does follow from an intelligent evaluation of the "interrelations" of events. Agricultural societies, for example, must rationalize at least part of the agricultural process, regardless of how much such rationalized action is supplemented by non-rationalized procedures. However, the basis of such rationalization is fundamentally different when traditionalism predominates as compared to when technicism prevails. As Marion Levy (1966) notes, "it is the essence of tradition that an action be justified as 'good' because it follows precedent, whereas it is the essence of rational action that a given end be attained by an adequate means." Moreover, continues Levy, "it may be possible to traditionalize rationality...but... in the face of changed (or changing) circumstances, the use of specific traditionalized means for a given end may well entail inadequate means and hence non-rational action." The crux of the matter is that technicism not only leads to the rationalization of social action as a consequence of empirical observation, but is prepared to continually evaluate both the means used and the ends sought on the basis of the same criteria. Thus a "qualified scientific observer" can accurately discern the nature of a social structure organized on the basis of technicism precisely because both those within that social structure and the outside observer are "defining the situation" from the same ontological and epistemological viewpoint.

The technicist as a socio-cultural engineer must be prepared to strip his image of society of that which is aesthetic or emotional. Society and its constituent parts are to be conceived as a complex machine which can be redesigned or adjusted at will. Those aesthetic, emotive, and irrational components of cultural life that are considered desirable, or necessary to maintain, must themselves be subjected to rational control lest in their manifestation, they impede the smooth operation of the socio-cultural machine.

Even man, a necessary and unpredictable component of that machine is to be "stabilized in his reactions by training and education, and all his newly acquired activities . . . coordinated according to a definite principle of efficiency within an organized framework" (Manheim 1940). The well-planned "spontaneous" mob demonstrations of today are bizzare examples of such rational organization of irrational sentiments to attain rational goals.

The technicist has an unbounded faith that through the application of carefully designed programs of technique, he will not only bring about the Good Society, but these programs will *be* the good society. The teleology of technicism is not external to the rational organization of society; this is its end. In this pursuit, it is bounded by nothing other than its calculus of efficiency. A Benthamite, utilitarian perception of social purpose may provide technicism with social legitimacy in fortuitous circumstances, but the technicist will push towards further technicalization of society even when such a process is of dubious cultural value. Technicism seeks always to determine its own mode of expression. One implication of this is that within developed societies production is no longer solely a function of meeting consumption needs. In these societies, the relationship is reversed: now consumption needs must be engineered (such as defining serviceable items as socially obsolescent, etc.).

No man, of course, is totally committed to the intellectual orientation of technicism, any more than any Muslim is committed to Islamic traditionalism. These ideational orientations have been drawn in bold outline for heuristic purposes and are to be understood essentially as Weberian "ideal-types." This is particularly necessary because of the fact that the modernizing elites (e. g. the Young Turks) in the Muslim world have continually articulated the nature of technicism in terms of modified traditionalism. As a result, the manifestation of these two ideational systems has been symbiotic in form, clouding their fundamental differences. This penchant on the part of the modernizing elites in this part of the world is only natural; to expect either these groups or the tradition-bound masses they address to break completely from the incubus of Islamic traditionalism would be to expect too much. Such an act would involve a *total* negation of the past—a past that constitutes an integral part of the identity pattern of each Muslim. The Turkish elite under Ataturk made an effort in this direction, but, as the events following the election of 1950 indicated, the influence of Islamic traditionalism was far from eradicated from the Turkish countryside by the Kemalist revolution (Frey 1965). (See also Chapter Nine for further discussion of this point). The failure of Kemalism to engineer that total metamorphosis of perception and behavior deemed necessary for sustained development was largely due to the fact that the Turkish modernizing elite of the period between the wars were themselves unable to recognize the syncretic mixture of technicism and traditionalism that made up the Kemalist ideology. Despite the fact that Islamic traditionalism and technicism have tended to be dialectically articulated in the form of contextually relevant syntheses, neither ideational system is amenable to permanent fusion with the other.

The initial impact of technicism on Islam, particularly in Turkey and Egypt, was inextricably interwoven with the military and political impact of the West itself. This was unfortunate in terms of later developmental efforts because the rationale for introducing technical modifications into the Muslim world assumed a negative and defensive character right from the very beginning. Analytically this period may be identified as that of the Islamic synthesis, a synthesis marked by the struggle of the traditional Islamic society to define the permissible scope of the technicist invasion while simultaneously striving to retain an intellectual grip on society. At the political level, measured steps were taken to use the fruits of technicism in selected sectors to strengthen the Muslim polity against further incursion of the technicist thinking. The military reforms of Sultan Selim III and Mahmud II in Turkey, as well as those of Mohammed Ali in Egypt, are examples of such sector modification. Similar reflections of this Islamic synthesis are to be found in the steps taken during the nineteenth century in Turkey in particular (Berkes 1964) to apply technicist thinking in the legal and administrative spheres so as to strengthen, rather than displace, traditional patterns.

While the spill-over effect of these institutional rationalizations produced some chain reaction with regard to other sectors of society, for over a century the intent of these reforms was less to effect any fundamental transformation of society than to preserve the remaining facets of the traditional culture. As a result, no systematic effort was made until quite recently to engender any universal transformation of the intellectual foundations of the Muslim society.

To those who could see beyond the more opportunistic adoption of technicist thinking, it was obvious that unsuccessful wars, capitulatory rights, restrictive commercial treaties, costly loans, and outright Western imperialism were not going to be stemmed until the weapon of the West—technicism—could find intellectual legitimacy within the traditional Islamic society.

The spokesman of the Islamic synthesis was Jamal-ad-Din as-Afghani (1839-1897). He called for a reformed Islam, an Islam that would not continue to provide legitimacy for the debilitating political and economic pattern of Islamic traditionalism. He advocated a re-opening of the gates of interpretation of Islamic dogma. He called for constitutional restraints on political leaders who were literally leasing their countries to Western powers under the guise of concessionary rights. He rejected the fatalism and social quietism of Islamic traditionalism, and called for the mobilization of all Islamic peoples in defense against Western political and economic penetration into the Muslim world.

Afghani's proposal to marry Western technicism with Islamic theology and morality only added another boost to the penetration of technicist thinking into the Muslim systems by giving to the technicist a cloak of legitimacy within the traditional Islamic context.

Moreover, the Islamic synthesis espoused by both Afghani and his disciple Mohammed Abduh (1849-1905) was further weakened by their focus on Pan-Islamism. Neither would accept a secularized definition of the political community. Their emphasis on the Islamic *umma* still finds expression in revitalized movements like the Muslim Brethren, but the rise of the nationalist synthesis has rendered such recurrent expressions anomalous to the contemporary mode of political organization within the Muslim world. The case of Turkey provides us with the best example of this. And it is to this case that I shall address myself in the following pages.

ISLAMIC LAW

CHAPTER FOUR

ISLAMIC LAW

LAW HAS BEEN defined in the following terms: "A social norm is legal if its neglect or infraction is regularly met, in threat or in fact, by the application of physical force by an individual or group possessing the socially recognized privilege of so acting" (Hoebel 1964: 28). Thus law is a system of social control having the object of regulating human conduct in accordance with certain rules. Different societies tend to develop different systems of social control; but law, which may be regarded as the "control of controls," is probably the best measure designed to protect what society honors. The magnitude of the legal edifice reflects the genius of its architects, but its survival down the centuries depends less on the legal structure than on the ability of succeeding generations to adapt it to new conditions of life (Hoebel 1964: 275). The attempt to change Islamic law, despite its notorious rigidity, which still has a strong hold on Muslim society, is worthy of close study. The following chapter provides a synthesis of Islamic law, with particular reference to its overriding features and its historical developmental dimensions. The question of its adaptability to new socio-cultural conditions is treated in Chapter Five, with regard to the organization of rules pertaining to the Muslim family in several Muslim countries.

"Obey God and His Prophet." In this Koranic command lies the supreme innovation introduced by Islam into the social structure of Arabia: The establishment of a novel political authority possessing legislative power. Law in classical Islamic theory is the revealed will of God, a divinely ordained system preceding and preceded by the Muslim state, controlling and controlled by Muslim society. There can thus be no notion of the law itself evolving as an historical phenomenon closely tied with the evolution of society and culture. Naturally the discovery and formulation of the divine law is a process of growth, systematically divided by traditional doctrine into several distinct stages. Master social planners, such as Omar (the second Caliph) were followed by interpreters who implemented his plans making their own particular contribution to it. But this process is seen in complete isolation from the cultural development of Islamic society as such. The role of the individual interpreter (jurist) is measured by the purely subjective standard of its intrinsic worth in the process of discovery of the divine command. It is not considered in the light of any external criteria or in its relationship to particular spatial and temporal cultural circumstances. In this sense the traditional picture of the growth of Islamic law completely lacks the dimension of historical-developmental depth.

Since direct access to revelation of the divine will have ceased upon the death of the Prophet Mohammed, the Sharia, having once achieved perfection of expression, was in principle static and immutable. Floating above Muslim society as a disembodied soul, freed from the currents and changing cultural conditions through time, it represented the eternally valid ideal towards which a society must aspire.

Inherent in Islamic law, to use the term in the sense of the laws which govern the lives of Muslims, is a distinction between the ideal doctrine and the actual practice, between the Sharia law as expounded by the classical jurist and the positive law administered by the courts; and this provides a convenient basis for anthropological-cultural inquiry, which would proceed simply along the lines of the extent to which the practice of the courts has coincided with or deviated from the norms of the Sharia. Literature on Islamic Law, however, has shown little interest in such an approach. Biographical chronicles of the judiciary in particular areas, description of non-Sharia jurisdictions and similar works are not lacking, but they cannot be regarded as even approaching a systematic analysis of Islam. Occasional protests against the legal practice by individual jurists and "Islamists" provide the exceptions to the general attitude of resignation which the majority has assumed. The standards of the religious law and the demands of political expediency often have not coincided; and perhaps the arbitrary power of the political authority has induced some jurists to adopt a discrete policy of ignoring rather than denying. But however that may be, the nature of literature on Muslim Law, coupled with absence of any system of "law-reporting," naturally makes any inquiry along the lines indicated a task of considerable difficulty. Light has been shed on certain aspects of the problem by Western scholarship, but the extent to which the ideal law has been translated into actuality in a given area at a given period remains a grave lacuna in our anthropological knowledge of the structure of Muslim society and Islamic Law.

Two developments in the present century, developments of wholly different origin and nature, but possessing, as will be seen, a departure of profound significance, require a radical revision of this traditional attitude. In the first place, Joseph Schacht (1964) has formulated a thesis of the origins of Sharia law which is irrefutable in its broad essentials and which proves that the classical theory of Sharia law was the outcome of a complex evolutionary process spanning a period of some three centuries. Further development of this thesis by Western scholarship has shown how closely the growth of Islamic law was linked to current socio-cultural, political, and economic conditions. In the second place, the notion of the Sharia as a rigid and immutable system has been propounded by sociologists (Levy 1959, Watt 1963) and also dispelled by others, primarily historians (Coulson, Bosworth) and others. In Turkey, Tunisia, Syria, particularly, the substance of Sharia family law, and in Soviet Central Asia, the overall structure of Islamic law as applied by the courts has been profoundly modified and to a large degree successfully adapted to the needs and the temper of changing cultural conditions.

When compared to legal systems based upon reason, Islam expressed as irrevocable will of Allah possesses two major characteristics: Firstly, it is a rigid and immutable system, embodying norms and values of an absolute and eternal validity which are not susceptible to modification by any legislative authority. Secondly, for the many different peoples and cultures which constitute the world of Islam, the divinely ordained Sharia represents the standard of uniformity against the variety of legal systems which would be the inevitable result if law were the product of human reason based upon the local circumstances and the particular needs of a given community. In so far then as the processual development of Sharia law falls, the processes may be measured in terms of these two criteria of rigidity and uniformity.

During the formative period of the seventh to the ninth centuries, diversity of legal doctrine in different regions of Islam was gradually reduced and the mobility of the law progressively restricted, as the movement towards the classical theory gained ground. In the tenth century, the law was cast in a rigid mold from which it still has not fully emerged. Of course, there are instances of differentially higher stages of emergence. Perhaps the degree of rigidity which the doctrine attained has been unduly exaggerated by some students of Islam, particularly in spheres other than that of the family laws; and the notion of a uniform Sharia is seriously qualified by wide variations of opinion between different schools and individual students of Islam from various disciplines. But a rift certainly developed between the precepts of the classical law and the varied and changing demands of Muslim society; and where the Sharia was unable to make the necessary accommodations, local customary law continued to prevail in practice, and the jurisdiction of non-Sharia tribunals was extended. From this fast approaching state of coma, attempts have been made to rouse and revive the Sharia by legal modernism.

Before going further, a distinction between modern and classical Islam is fundamental. According to the classical tradition, law is imposed from above and postulates the eternally valid standards to which the structure of state and society must conform. In the modernist or reformed approach, law is shaped by the needs of society; its function is to answer constantly arising social problems. But Islamic legal modernism or reform in fact represents an interesting amalgam of the two positions. Social engineering is a fitting description of reform activists and movements. Yet the needs and aspirations of a culture cannot be, in Islam (especially in the *Sunni* doctrine), the exclusive determinants of law; they can legitimately operate only within the bounds of the norms and principles irrevocably established by the divine command. And it is precisely the determination of these limits which is the unfinished task of meaningful cultural-legal transformations.

The clash, therefore, between the allegedly rigid dictates of the traditional law and the demands of modern society poses for Islam a fundamental problem of principle. If the law is to retain its form as the expression of the divine command, if indeed it is to remain Islamic law, reforms cannot be justified on the ground of cultural necessity per se; they must find their juristic basis and support in principles which are Islamic in the sense that they are endorsed, expressly or implied, by the divine will. As long as the theory of classical Muslim jurisprudence was predominant such support was difficult to find. Here it is, then, that the connection between modern legal activities and the results of the researches of Western orientalists becomes readily apparent.

In its extreme form, legal modernism rests upon the notion that the will of God was never expressed in terms so rigid or comprehensive as the classical doctrine maintained, but that it enunciates broad general principles which admit of varying interpretations and varying applications according to the circumstances of the time. Modernism, therefore, is a movement towards an historical interpretation of the divine revelation. Islamic scholars (Schacht 1964, Levy 1957, Watt 1961, Gibb 1955, Von Grunebaum 1955) have demonstrated that Sharia law originated as the implementation of the precepts of divine revelation within the framework of current cultural conditions, and thus provide the basis of historical fact to support the ideology underlying legal modernism. Once the classical theory is seen in its historical perspective, as implying a stage in the evolution of the Sharia, modernist activities no longer appear as a "total" departure from the one legitimate position, but preserve the continuity of Islamic legal tradition by taking up again the attitude of the earliest jurists and reviving a corpus whose growth had been artificially arrested and which had laid dormant for a period of about ten centuries.

Modernist activities gauged for accelerated and positive culture change, therefore, can find their most solid foundation, in a critical appreciation of the historical growth of Sharia law. As this movement gathers momentum and as the need for change (through external and internal pressures) becomes acute, a new era shall and must be ushered in.

Prior to the advent of Islam, the unit of society in Arabia was a confederation of clans or large lineages (tribe), the group of blood relatives who claimed descent from a common ancestor. It was to the tribe as a whole, not merely to its nominal leader, that the individual owed allegiance, and it was from the tribe as a whole that he obtained the protection of his interests. The exile, or any person hapless enough to find himself outside the sphere of this collective responsibility and security, was an outlaw in the fullest sense of the term, his prospects of survival remote unless he succeeded in gaining admittance into a tribal group by a process of adoption of affiliation known as *wala* (Smith 1903).

To the tribe as a whole belonged the power to determine the standard by which its members should live. But here the tribe is conceived not merely as the group of its present representatives but as a historical-cultural entity embracing past, present, and future generations. And this notion, of course, is the basis of the recognition of customary law. The tribe was bound by the body of unwritten rules which had evolved along with the historical growth of the tribe itself as the manifestation of its total structure and character. Neither the tribal *shaykh* nor any representative assembly had legislative power to interfere with the system. Modification or change of the law, which naturally occurred with the passage of time, may have been initiated by individuals, but their real source lay in the will and outlook of the whole community, for they could not form part of the tribal law unless and until they were generally accepted as such.

In the absence of any legislative authority, it is not surprising that there did not exist any official organization for the adminis-

tration of the law. Enforcement of the law was generally the
responsibility of the private individual who had suffered injury.
The tribal code usually demanded that inter-tribal disputes be
settled by force of arms, while within the tribe they would usually
be handled by arbitration (Smith 1903). But again, this function
was not exercised by appointed officials. A suitable ad hoc arbi-
trator (*hakam*) was chosen by the parties to the dispute, a popular
choice being the *kahin*, a priest of a pagan cult who claimed super-
natural powers of divination.

This general picture of the early customary tribal law of Arabia
in the sixth century requires some qualification as regards the
settled communities of Mecca and Medina. Mecca, the birth-
place of the Prophet Mohammed and a flourishing center of trade,
possessed a commercial law of sorts, while Medina, an agricultural
area, knew elementary forms of land tenure (Watt 1961). In
Mecca, moreover, there appears to have existed the rudiments of
a system for legal administration. Public arbitrators were appointed and other officials were charged with the task of recovering
compensation in cases of homicide or wounding. Yet in both these
centers, just as among the Bedouin tribes, the sole basis of law lay
in its recognition as established customary practice.

The year A.D. 622 saw the establishment of the Muslim community
in Medina. The Arab tribes or sub-tribes (with some temporary
exceptions) accepted Mohammed as the Prophet or spokesman of
God, and regarded themselves and his Meccan followers as cons-
tituting a group of a new kind wherein the bond of a common
religious faith transcended tribal ties. While Mohammed's position developed into one of political and legal sovereignty, the will
of God as transmitted to the community by him in the Koranic
revelations came to supercede tribal custom in various respects.
To assess the nature and scope of the legislation which the Koran
contains and its impact upon the form and substance of the existing customary law is the purpose of the remainder of this chapter.

In the evolution of a society the technical process of legislation
is a secondary stage. Reducing into terms of right and obligation
an accepted standard of conduct and behavior, and providing
measures in the event of its infringements, it presupposes the existence of this accepted standard. Therefore, the religious message

of the founder-Prophet of Islam, the purpose of which included the establishing of certain basic standards of behavior for the Muslim community, precedes, both in point of time and emphasis, his role as a political legislator. Accordingly, the so-called legal matter of the Koran consists mainly of broad and general propositions as to what the aims and aspirations of Muslim society and culture should be. It is essentially the bare formulation of the Islamic religious state.

Most of the basic notions underlying technologically modern society find such a mode of expression in the Koran acceptable in a general sense. Compassion for the culturally deprived members of society, commercial enterprise, incorruptibility in the administration of justice are all enjoined as desirable behavioral ideals, without being translated into any legal structure of rights and duties. The same applies to many precepts which are more particular and more peculiarly Islamic, in their terms. Drinking of alcoholic beverages and usury are both simply declared to be forbidden (*haram*) in practically the same terms. But no indication of the legal incidence of the practices is contained in the Koran. In fact, drinking alcohol later became a criminal offense punishable by flogging (Rahman 1966) while usury was a purely civil matter, the transaction being a type of invalid or unenforceable contract. This clearly demonstrates the distinct attitudes of the religious prophet and the political legislator. Both are obviously concerned with the consequences in terms of practical sanctions enforceable by human agencies, the prophet sees them as the attainment of merit or fault in the sight of Allah. The ultimate sanction visualized for the infringement of the Koranic provisions is always the blessing or wrath of God. For example, those who wrongfully exploit the property of orphans, says the Koran, "only shall burn in the flame." While political legislation considers social problems in terms of the effects of an individual's behavior upon his neighbor or upon the community as a whole, a religious law looks beyond this to the effect that actions may have upon the conscience of the one who performs them (Gibb 1947). In short, the primary purpose of the Koran is to regulate not the relationship of man to his society, but his relationship with his creator.

While the Koranic legislation is predominantly ethical in quality, the quantity is not great by any standards. It amounts in all to some six hundred verses and the vast majority of these are concerned with the religious duties and ritual practices of prayer, fasting and pilgrimage. No more than approximately eighty verses deal with legal topics in the strict sense of the term. The first laws of a society are naturally couched in brief and simple terms—as was the case with the Twelve Tables of Roman Law. But unlike the Twelve Tables, the Koran does not attempt to cover, in however rudimentary a form, all the basic elements of a given legal relationship. Although the regulations which are of a more specifically legal tone cover a great range of behavior, ranging from women's dress to the division of the spoils of war, and from the prohibition of certain flesh to the penalty of flogging for fornication, they often have the appearance of ad hoc solutions for particular problems rather than attempts to deal with a broad and general spectrum of behavior.

This piecemeal nature of the legislation follows naturally perhaps from the circumstances in which the Koran was "revealed"; for the official compilation of the Koran, which did not appear until some years after the death of the Prophet, represents an arbitrary arrangement of short passages which had been uttered by the Prophet at various times and in various places throughout his lifetime—or at least, as far as the legal verses are concerned, during the ten years of his residence at Medina. An example of this type of regulation which catered for the exigencies of the moment is provided by the Verse 37 which abolishes the pre-Islamic custom of adoption, under which an adopted child had the legal status of the adopter's own child; for this was so designed to settle the controversy which arose from the marriage of the Prophet to the divorced wife of his adopted son Zayd (Watt 1961). Similarly, the Koranic verses which lay down the penalty of eighty lashes for the offense of a false accusation of unchastity (*qadhf*) were revealed following imputations of adultery against the Prophet's wife Aisha.

Certain topics, it is true, are dealt with at considerable length. But even here there is no single comprehensive exposition of the topic. It was simply that certain problems of a recurring nature gave rise to a series of regulations, disjoined in point both of time and substance, on the same general subject, and these, when gathered together from their various positions in the Koran, afford some semblance of a detailed treatment. Without doubt it is the general subject of the position of women, married women in particular, which occupies the most important position in the Koranic law. Rules on marriage and divorce are numerous and varied. With their general objective of the improvement of women's status, they represent some of the most radical reforms of pre-Islamic Arabian customary law effected in the Koran. The importance of two outstanding rules in this context may be briefly discussed.

As regards marriage, the Koran commands that the wife alone shall receive the dowry (*mahr*) payable by the husband. While payments to the wife herself were sometimes made in pre-Islamic times, the basic concept of marriage under customary law was that of a sale of the woman by her father, or other near male relative, who received the purchase price paid by the husband. The effect of this Koranic rule then, is to transfer the wife from the position of sale object to that of a contracting party who, in return for her granting the right of sexual union with herself, is entitled to receive the due consideration of the dower. She is now endowed with a legal competence she did not possess before.

In the laws of divorce the supreme innovation of the Koran lies in the introduction of the "waiting period" (*idda*). Prior to Islam, a husband could discard his wife at a moment's notice. His repudiation (*talag*) of his wife, a right naturally stemming from his position as a purchaser of her, operated as an immediate and final severance of the marital relationship. The Koran now virtually suspended the effect of the repudiation until the expiration of the "waiting period," which was to last until the wife had completed three menstrual cycles or, if she proved pregnant, until delivery of the child. This period is primarily designed, according to the express terms of the Koran itself, to provide an opportunity for reconciliation, and during it the wife is entitled to financial support from the husband.

Reforms such as these obviously go a long way towards ameliorating the position of the wife. But they are so designed to remedy only particular aspects of the marital relationship. They do not attempt to create an entirely novel structure of family law or to eradicate the basic concepts of existing customary practices. Marriage remains a contract in which the husband, as quasi-purchaser, occupies the dominant position. He also retains his basic right to unilaterally terminate the marriage. "The men are overseers over the women," says the Koran, "by reason of the property which they have contributed (dowry and maintenance)." But this patriarchal scheme of society is now subjected to the tempering influence of the ethical standard of fair treatment for women. The often-repeated injunction to "retain wives honorably or release them with kindness" finds its practical implementation in legal rules which mitigate for women the rigors of that society and remove its harshest features. In short, the Koranic regulations modify in certain particulars rather than supplant entirely the existing customary law.

Perhaps the best illustration of the various aspects of the Koranic laws to which I have referred is provided by the regulations concerning inheritance. In pre-Islamic times the rules of inheritance were designed to consolidate the strength of the individual tribe as an effective participant in the activities of warfare. Patrilineal in structure, the tribe was formed of those who traced descent from the common ancestor exclusively through male links. Accordingly, in order to keep property within the tribe, rights of inheritance obtained solely to the male agnate relatives of the deceased. Furthermore, it was the nearest such relative alone who inherited, the order of priority being the descendants of the deceased, followed by his father, his brothers, and their descendants, his paternal grandfather, and finally his uncles and their descendants. Although there is some evidence that property was occasionally bequeathed, outside to close relatives such as daughters and parents, the general rule was that females had no rights of succession; nor had minor children (Schacht 1964) on the ground presumably, of their inability to participate in military activities and war.

The first Koranic reference to this subject is a typically ethical injunction which urges a person who is on the point of death to "bequeath equitably to his parents and kindred." This provision obviously qualifies, in general, the system of exclusive inheritance by the male agnate relatives and in particular recognizes the capacity of women relatives to succeed. As such, it reflects the transition effected by Islam from a society based on blood relationship to one based on common religious faith; and in this new society, the individual family has replaced the tribe as the basic social unit.

Later circumstances, however, necessitated the translation of this general injunction into more positive and practical rules. Following the death of many Muslims in the battles fought against the "unbelievers," a series of Koranic "revelations" allotted specific fractions of the deceased's estate to individual relatives. Of the nine relatives so entitled, six are women (Levy 1957)—the wife, the mother, the daughter, grand-daughter, consanguine and uterine sisters—and the remaining three are male relatives who would either never have inherited at all under the old system, that is, the husband and the uterine brothers, or would have been excluded by a nearer agnate, that is, the father who would not have inherited in competition with a son of the deceased. Although the Koran does not expressly recognize the claims of the male agnate relatives as such, it enacts that where the deceased is survived by sons and daughters, the share of the son shall be double that of the daughter; and a similar principle applies when the heirs are the deceased's brothers and sisters.

The obvious intention then of the Koranic rules is not to sweep away the agnatic system entirely but merely to modify it, with the particular objective of improving the position of the female relatives, by superimposing upon the male agnates an additional class of new heirs. Once again, the legislation is by way of a supplement to, not a substitute for, the existing customary law.

For those who were pledged to conduct their lives in accordance with the will of God, the Koran itself did not provide a simple and straightforward code of law. As a legislative document, the Koran raises many problems, but I am not for the moment concerned with the manifold and complex questions of the interpretation of the Koran and its precise implications which were to occupy the minds of later generations. There were, however, two basic problems which must have been of immediate concern to the contemporaries of the Prophet themselves.

In the first place there was the question of the effect, in terms of practical measures, of the essentially ethical standards established by the Koran. Usury had been simply prohibited, but it is hardly too cynical to suggest that the potential lender or borrower might be at least as interested in the effect of his dealing on his pocket or his person as he would be in the prospect of eternal damnation.

In some cases, the legal implications of an ethical norm were self-evident. On the subject of homicide and physical assaults, for example, the Koran lays down the standard of just retribution in the maxim "an eye for an eye and a life for a life." Under the pre-Islamic customary law, a rough system of private justice, dominated by the notion of vengeance, had prevailed in these matters. The loss of a tribal member was to be avenged by the infliction of a corresponding loss upon the culprit's tribe who were collectively responsible for the action of one of their members.

Until satisfactory vengeance had been effected, the soul of the victim could not rest in peace, and since the usual tendency was for a tribe to set an exaggerated value on the member it had lost, two or more lives might be claimed in revenge for a single victim. The Koranic maxim thus radically altered the legal incidence of homicide. Henceforth only one life—the life of the killer himself was due for the life of the victim, and the distinction is marked by a change of terminology, the term *tha'r* (blood revenge) being replaced by that of *qisas* (justice retaliation). It is once again noteworthy, however, that the basic structure of the existing law is unchanged. Homicide remains an offense which falls into the category of civil injuries rather than that of public offenses or crimes, for it is the relatives of the victim who have the right to demand retaliation, accept compensation or pardon the offense altogether. It is still a matter of private justice, but the justice is now to be meted out in accordance with the moral standard of just reparation for loss suffered, the maxim of a life for a life itself stemming from the broader religious principle that all Muslims are equal in the sight of God.

But the legal implications of the Koranic precepts were by no means always as self-evident as in the case of homicide. Polygyny, restricted to a maximum of four wives concurrently, is expressly permitted, but at the same time husbands are enjoined to treat the co-wives equally and not to marry more than one wife if they fear they will be unable to do so. Does this represent a legal condition attaching to polygynous unions, and if so, what is the remedy for its breach? Or is the duty of impartial treatment simply a matter for the conscience of the individual husband? These and similar questions would soon require an answer from those whose task it is to apply the "law of God."

The second and even more obvious problem arises from the omissions in the Koranic legislation. On many legal topics, of course, the Koran is completely silent. But this would occasion no difficulty, at least for the early Muslim community, inasmuch as the existing customary law would continue to apply in these respects. It is a natural canon of construction, and one in full accord with the general tenor of the Koran, that the *status quo* is tacitly ratified unless it is expressly amended. Again, the rules in the Koran on certain subjects may be extremely rudimentary. There is the repeated injunction, for example, to pay alms (*zakat*), to the extent a person can afford, to those in need. Simple rules like this naturally proved inadequate as society progressed, and they were later developed into an elaborate system of taxation which specified the amount payable, the property subject to the tax and order of priority among beneficiaries. But this does not constitute an omission, in the sense that I use the term, in the Koran. Nevertheless, in certain respects the Koran formulated novel rules which were manifestly incomplete in themselves. An outstanding instance is provided by the rules of inheritance previously discussed. While the injunction to make out bequests in favor of near relatives had clearly been superseded by the system of fixed shares, this begged the obvious and unanswered question as to whether any power at all of testamentary disposition still remained, and if it did, to what extent and in favor of whom could it be exercised.

How these gaps were filled, and how the same problems which have been referred to here were solved, will be indicated in chapters that follow. Here an attempt has been made at an objective assessment of the Koran itself as a legislative document, and enough has now been said to show that it does not expressly

provide solutions for all the legal problems inherent in the organization of Muslim societies and cultures. The principle that God
was the only law-giver and that his command was to have supreme
control over all aspects of life was clearly established. But that
command was not expressed in the form of a complete or comprehensive charter for the Muslim community. Later events, indeed,
were to show that the Koranic precepts form little more than the
preamble to an Islamic code of cultural behavior for which succeeding generations did and should apply rational operative parts.

THE ORGANIZATION OF ISLAM:
AN HISTORICAL ACCOUNT

CHAPTER FIVE

THE ORGANIZATION OF ISLAM:
AN HISTORICAL ACCOUNT

ANY STUDY OF transformation must begin at the beginning of change. In the case of Islam, there is a special profit to be gained from contrasting the Islamic past and present. Traditional Islam, like modern Islam, was a society almost continually beset with rivalries, assassinations, wars, and rebellions. Yet it survived over large areas as a single socio-cultural system and always as an interrelated pattern of faith and action for nearly 1300 years. What was the secret of its extraordinary endurance amid almost constant instability? Why is a system that has proven itself so resilient in the past faced by inadaptability today?

An attempt to answer these questions in the first part of this inquiry may help to ·define with greater precision the character and scope of the forces of change which challenge the Muslim social systems. Only by understanding the past will we be able to see why the cost and pain of change (or of avoiding change) runs so high in the Muslim world.

It is appropriate to begin with the birth of Islam, for its official calendar starts not with the birth of its Prophet Mohammed but with Islam's first political act—the founding of the Community of Believers in A.D. 622.

Divine and therefore perfect, perfect and therefore complete, complete and therefore final, final and therefore unalterable. Such was the constitution that Prophet Mohammed received for the Moslem community. It was a constitution that did not separate the realm of Allah from the realm of rulers on earth, or the realm of ethics from the realm of law. As detailed in the Koran and the Sharia, the corpus of Islamic jurisprudence, Allah's realm was not circumscribed. His word covered with equal authority matters of worship, ritual, politics, economics, and personal relations. By conducting himself in conformity with this established pattern of righteousness, the Muslim could hope to establish a perfect society on earth.

The term Islam designates, therefore, not only a religion, as mentioned earlier but also a community and a way of life. For the first time in Arab history, this community transcended the tribe, for it is composed of all who are ready to surrender themselves to the same God ("Muslims" are those who have surrendered themselves to Allah, "Islam" is this state of surrender). Its ruler's supreme purpose is to execute Allah's revealed law, being himself subject to it. Its learned men exert themselves to understand the law, and advise both the ruler and the ruled in its meaning.

Such is the vision of Islam held by the "ulema," literally the "knowers," the scholar-legist of the Islamic code of conduct. Until the nineteenth century, all their books and teachings were based on this view. In the twentieth century, Muslims who think and write nostalgically about the past recall that world. In fact, it never existed.

The conduct of righteous politics proved to be no easier for Muslims than for other peoples. The Islamic attempt began as an inspired response to great needs. Arabia in the seventh century heard prophets mourning the multiplicity of faiths while men tired of the constant warring among tribes in the absence of a clearly transcendant authority (Smith 1903). But the Prophet Mohammed alone was inspired to establish a Community of Believers that would permanently overcome moral and political instability in a society organized to serve Allah. He succeeded in laying the emotional, intellectual, legal, and political foundations for a new social system that was to endure for over a millennium. But it was not quite the community he had in mind.

The new community was born in compromise. Mohammed, who had been forced to leave his Meccan tribe, the Quraish, in order to find support as a prophet elsewhere, had initially organized his followers in a brotherhood divorced from all regional and tribal allegiances. The great majority who became Muslims in Mohammed's lifetime and thereafter, however, were not individual converts, but families and tribes who made the decision to join the larger community of Islam on the basis of their own customary solidarity (Watt 1961). Alongside the demand for the unity of all Believers, there were thus, from the first, these other organized and competing claims for loyalty.

The new community of Islam never acquired institutions that could permanently resolve such conflicts of loyalty and the constant battle for power which this multiplicity of allegiances entailed. Of the four Caliphs who succeeded Mohammed, only the first died a natural death. In retrospect, orthodox Muslims remember them as the four pious Caliphs. There is, of course, the disagreement between the Shi'a and Sunni sects in regard to who should have been the first to succeed Mohammed. The Shi'a contend that Ali was the legitimate heir by virtue of his close kin ties with the Prophet, while the Sunnis argue that Abu-Bakr was the choice of the community by consensus. The first four Caliphs were succeeded by the Umayyad branch of the Prophet's tribe, which reasserted its ancient political pre-eminence in Mecca to become the first dynasty of Islam. Within a hundred years after the Prophet's death, the Umayyad dynasty expanded Islam into an area reaching from France to the Indus, larger than the Roman Empire at its zenith, but at the cost of turning the new Community of Believers into an Arab Empire. ''For many centuries after the Muslim conquest, the vast majority of the Caliphs' subjects were not Sunni 'Islamic orthodox,' and hated Sunnism as the emblem of an oppressive regime and a foreign privileged ruling class of Arabs'' (Lewis 1937 : 22).

The Umayyad dynasty was overthrown toward the beginning of

the second Islamic century by the Abbasids, another branch of Mohammed's tribe, who led a movement to re-fashion the Arab Empire into a Muslim Empire. The dream of a Community of Believers united to carry out Allah's laws never ceased to inspire Muslims and to stimulate action to turn this vision into a reality. But all such efforts, including that of the Abbasids, produced new rivalries and discontents, splintering Islam in the task of creating unity. Perhaps only a community that experienced so much disunity and lawlessness would hold on so dearly for so long to the ideal of a Community of Believers joined under divine law.

Certainly the environment of South-West Asia and North Africa itself was inhospitable to movements of unity. This region of the world has never resembled the neat cluster of well-articulated colored blocks that map-makers draw. Most of the population live in a scattering of large and small oases, far separated from each other by high, rugged mountains and broad deserts. However, absolute was the Caliph in Baghdad or Constantinople, his powers of supervision and execution diminished almost geometrically with the distance from the capital. The thin coastal oases of Morocco, Algeria and Tunisia were in their entire Islamic history of 1250 years united with the Arab (Muslim) Empire to the east for only about 100 years; only twice, for about 120 years altogether, was it united with a single North African empire. Egypt, mostly desert but containing one of the most reliable sources of water, was usually strong enough to assert its autonomous political existence within any Islamic Empire.

Segmented geographic isolation and sharp competition for scarce resources helped to perpetuate that spirit of separatism and rivalry, which in most conflicts, elevated the kinship of common blood above the kinship of common faith. Traditional Islam did not succeed in developing sufficient spiritual and material resources to alter this environment. It could not establish institutions above the kinship group that could assure the continuance of any particular state, provide for the equal application of authority in all its parts, or cease the peaceful transfer of power.

Traditional Islam gave an appearance of continuity and stability that was deceiving. For six hundred years, it is true, a single family supplied all the sultans for the Ottoman Empire, the largest and most enduring Islamic state. In fact, however, power in the Ottoman Empire was usually shared among various autonomous groups and rulers. Between the late eighteenth and early nineteenth century, for example, one finds Egypt pursuing its customary independent course, and Iraq supporting its own Mamluk dynasty (from 1749-1831). Also there were other independent ruling groups governing Damascus and Jerusalem. It would be "monotonous and repetitious," writes one historian, "to describe each one of these petty lords ruling autonomously within the Ottoman Empire and to relate the incidents of his rise to power and his local tyrannies" (Fisher 1959: 254).

Islam would have scarcely survived for so long as a political system and as a contributing civilization, however, if its longevity had depended only on the uncertainties of petty tyranny. Its survival is all the more remarkable in view of many threats from outside.

Over three hundred years ago, the Islamic world was already almost encircled by the superior strength and enterprise of Western sailors and soldiers and Russian Cossacks. "The noose was round the victims' neck," writes Arnold Toynbee. He goes on further (Toynbee 1954: 8: 219-222) to state that the victim

had by then already been foiled in diverse attempts to break out of the toil. This failure was a signal one in view of his possession of the interior lines. . .and he was now inexorably condemned to die by strangulation whenever an alien executioner might choose to draw the fatal bow-string tight. . . .Why had both the West and Russia been so slow in taking the offensive against an hereditary enemy at their gates? And why, after they had at last tasted blood, had they not managed to devour more than the extremities of this Tityos' carcass? In a list of reasons for the Islamic world's rather surprising reprieve we may include the initial self-confidence with which the Muslims had been inspired by the memory of the extraordinary previous achievements; the subsequent tactical victories had masked their strategical defeat in their attempts to break out of the toils of Western and Russian encirclement; the long-lasting effect of these impressive Muslim successes in including Westerners to take the Muslims at their own valuation; the leading modern Western peoples' loss of interest in the Mediterranean for some three hundred years after their conquest of the ocean towards the close of the fifteenth century; and the mutual frustration of the rival competitors for the spoils of the Islamic World after the Western Powers and Russia had at last become aware that the once formidable titan now lay at their mercy.

These are valid points, but it would be misleading to write an exposition of Islamic society merely as the tale of divorce between vision and power, and accredit its long endurance to an accident of good fortune. This is not the whole truth any more than is the argument that Islam was one perfect moment in history foiled, according to one's lights, by secular lusts of the latter Umayyad or Abbasid dynasties, the cultural destruction wreaked by an invading Turkic and Mongol hordes, the weakness and errors of later Ottomans, or the encroachments òf the "imperialist" West. To understand the traditional Islamic system, one must see it in its entirety, not merely as a turbulent sequence of events or as a compendium of its most glorious or desperate cultural past.

Each of the main participants in the Islamic system, sultans, scholar-legists, saint, soldier, tribesman, villager, intellectual, and devotee of religious "brotherhoods" called himself "Muslim." In one sense, this was a valid identification. Each lived under conditions created by the presence of the others; all roles were entwined in a single pattern of action and norms. Yet, in another sense, this identification was misleading. Far more than the medieval European or the traditional Japanese, every Muslim also retained his spiritual, political, and social autonomy. Despite its original ideal, Islam had many faces, for what was demanded of each Muslim in practice was not theological or political conformity. The decisive criterion of membership in community was acquiescence in the largely unwritten code which defined the rules of social conduct and norms. The Muslim community hoped for, but rarely ever insisted on, other rules that marked an individual as a believer.

Traditional Islam survived for more than a millennium in a harsh and uncertain environment because it was capable of converting constant tension and conflict into a force for constant political renewal and cultural survival. This extraordinary cultural and social system of organization, mobile in all its parts yet static as a whole, is rare in human-cultural systems for its endurance. This resilient system has been one of the traditional Islam's greatest, yet least understood features. The Islamic system's ability to convert tensions into balances deserves closer examination, both for the sake of developing a theory of cultural change that reflects the actual practice of the traditional Islamic system and for the sake of understanding why such a system could not continue to function in the modern age (Rosenthal 1958).

Most Muslims have lived and died in the small, closed kinship group of the family and the tribe. Whatever the original motive for conversion to Islam, whether piety, fear, profit, or politics, the folk Muslim community could find in the Islamic way of life a broader, more profound understanding of ultimate and secular imperatives, and a larger scope for political and social mobility than it had usually possessed before.

Still, its relationship to the Islam of the Caliphs or scholar-legists remained uneasy. Folk Islam (equivalent to Redfield's "small tradition") could appreciate Caliphs as enforcers of the larger code ("the great tradition") of revelation and conduct, and of peace among settled and nomadic tribes. There were advantages in the rule of a sacred stranger who could bring peace and justice, but a stranger by his very existence did not fit into the consensus of kin, and therefore was bound to inspire fear and suspicion no less than awe and respect. Even the kinship group's own leaders could not command or legislate in defiance of the existing tribal consensus (Watt 1961). A secular-minded sultan who ruled by exploiting rivalries and represented neither kin nor the large code was an obvious menace. The early splintering of the new Community of Believers renewed the threat of unprincipled external authority to the integrity of the kinship group. As a result, a considerable number of families, villages, and tribes sought parochial isolation in the mountain strongholds or desert vastness. For most, however, there was little security. The very existence of a multiple of kinship groups in an environment of great scarcity, of unstable centralized power, and the absence of any intervening, stable, powerful, property-owning class were permanent incitements of tribal imperialism. Islam provided a new cause or rationalization for conquest. The splintering of Islam allowed all manner of men to assert the resuscitation of Islam as their justification for building their own empires, without in fact heeding their moral ties with all Believers.

One of the greatest Arab sociologists and historians, Ibn Khaldun (1332-1406), has analysed the doom of continuous rise and decline of all such caliphates, sultanates, and kingships in a fashion applicable to the entire period of traditional Islam, including its last remnants in contemporary Saudi Arabia and Yemen (Khaldun 1958:I:252-286). When a tribe found itself blessed with more *asabiyah* (loyalty, courage, and will based on strong group solidarity) than any neighboring tribe, it would move out to conquer. Conquest by force or the threat of force was the only way in which a state could be formed. A tribe was organized by lines of obligations of blood. In a patriarchal egalitarianism, it required no institutions of state. A state involved control over men with whom one had no automatic kinship ties. Hence to form a state meant to form an empire, and thus create a new and uncertain pattern of dominance and submission. Each conquered tribe sought to the utmost to protect its integrity for the sake of survival and for future struggles for predominance.

The conqueror himself, according to Ibn Khaldun, was secure in his rule because he had defeated others and had enlarged the respect of his tribe by virtue of his victory and the distribution of booty. The son who succeeded him could not claim the respect due to a victor; he usually demonstrated his prowess by building monuments and encouraging luxury, and secured his power by finding allies in many parts of his empire. Since his own tribe was no longer fit for war, yet being closest to him was most prone to produce rivals, the king began to rely increasingly on mercenaries. As a result, *asabiyah* that united him with his tribe weakened. The grandson, having to his credit neither conquest nor construction, became the tool of the mercenary army, the only local group with force at its command, or else fell prey to conquest by a tribe with a stronger *asabiyah*.

Whether in the three generations, a dozen generations, or a

single one, this scheme covers the history of all parts of the Islamic world. Wisdom, energy, imagination, and shrewdness have sometimes allowed a particular leader to delay the doom spelled by Ibn Khaldun. There were clear-cut limits, however. The sources of wealth, including booty, tribute, taxes, trade, and harvests were circumscribed and uncertain, and the ruler sought to marshal them for the uses of his dynasty. In the most illustrious phases of Islamic history, schools, hospitals, mosques, as well as writing and art, experienced the ruler's patronage, as did, in the darkest periods, the military commander, the torturers and the executioners. Solicitude for the material well-being of his subjects as a whole, however, was required neither by the Sharia nor by sultanic tradition. Defense against the political power of unbelievers, the administration of the Islamic code of Justice and enforcement of public morality were the only duties prescribed for the ruler by the Sharia and even the fulfilment of these obligations often suffered due to weakness, intra-Muslim rivalries, and expediency. The bureaucracy was appointed to function only as an extension of the sultan's person. The soldiery were, while he remained strong enough to control them, the sultan's personal property or personal henchmen, without permanent links to state or society.

For most of his subjects, the sultan's power was thus absolute but almost irrelevant. The Caliph Mamun (813-833 A.H.), though himself one of the most liberal and philosophical of rulers, is quoted as saying: "The best life has he who has an ample house, a beautiful wife, and sufficient means, who does not know us and whom we do not know" (Grunebaum 1955:26). "It should perhaps be noted," Grunebaum adds (1955: 136), "that despite theoretical differences and actual hostilities between Sunnite and Shi'ite governments, their administrative practices would seem to have been more or less the same."

Yet this is not the full story of rise, conflict, decay, and renewal in Islam. Seldom was the struggle between kinship group and supra-tribal authority merely political. Even in its political disunity, Islam remained a transcending bond among kinship groups, though not in the way that had originally been intended—by fostering an undivided political loyalty in Mohammed's caliphs. Instead, by placing all loyalties and relationships under the authority of (one)

Allah, Islam reinforced a more ancient test of political legitimacy
—the ruler's ability to protect the moral and physical integrity of
society's most immediate and enduring dimension, the kinship
group.

Even before the coming of Islam, the kinship groups of South-
West Asia had long acted on the implicit assumption that faith and
community constituted a single web. This web was composed
exclusively of personal relationships—whether to neighbor, nature,
or spirits. Any ruler, whether imposed lord or the kinship group's
own victorious chieftain could justify his status only by his success
in his personal relationships, whether with his own group or with
ultimate powers, including Allah. He might be blamed for the
drought no less than the taxes.

After the coming of Islam, kinship groups continued to grant
their full loyalty only in personal relationships, now reinforced by
Allah's final standard for judging such relationships. More than
ever before, rebellion seemed to be a duty whenever the ruler, by
either impiety or injustice, morally isolated himself from the
community.

In seeking to set the world in tune again with the moral laws of
the universe, the kinship groups often linked themselves with a
movement equally devoted to personal relationships–the "religious
brotherhoods." While many scholar-legists, as guardians and
interpreters of the Orthodox Islam, became defenders of caliphal
and sultanic authority, large numbers of Muslims bound themselves to each other in brotherhoods dedicated to personal unity
with Allah and with ritual brothers. These brotherhoods took
various forms (Lewis 1937: 23-27). Some were craft and trade
guilds dedicated to the autonomous regulation of the spiritual,
economic and, whenever possible, political welfare of their members.
Some fraternal organizations, by their devotion to contemplation,
ecstatic exercises, or mutual assistance, helped to make acquiescence to superior power bearable. Others were openly or covertly
organized as fighters for "virtue." Between the ninth and twelfth
centuries, several brotherhoods took the form of Ismaili heresies which by their religio-political rebellions kept the Ismailic
realm in constant turmoil, and succeeded in establishing several
major rival centers of power. The largest and most enduring

of them, the Fatimid Caliphate in Egypt (971-1173 A.H.), was at least the equal in power and prosperity of the orthodox caliphate of Baghdad (Lewis 1940 : 43-63).

Like conquest inspired by tribal *asabiyah*, rebellions inspired by religio-political mysticism served not only to destroy existing authority in Islam, but also continued to renovate it. All successful rebellions produced states. All states, in turn, inspired new rebellions. The rebellions and state-forming activities of the religious brotherhoods continued to the nineteenth century, when the Mahdi Mohammed Ahmad created a state in the Sudan and the Sanusi a state in Cyrenaica.

In the first two centuries of Islam, the ulema had been courageous and creative in trying to avoid a divorce between law, morality, and politics by expanding and revising the unalterable constitution Allah had revealed to the community (Schacht 1950; Khadduri and Liebesny 1955). An empire needed governing, and on this subject, the Koran was silent, inadequate, or too restrictive in many fields. By relying as guides first on the sayings and actions of the Prophet, then of his companions (apostles), and finally on the invention of such sayings and actions (including the invented saying of Mohammed, "Whatever is good I said it," and his invented reassurance that "My community will not agree on error") and on the actual customary law of the conquered areas, the ulema greatly expanded the available corpus of law. So powerful had been the impact of the original revelation, however, that the four schools of Islamic jurisprudence (to be discussed in a later chapter) which emerged during the first 200 years differed relatively little in spirit or detail.

Yet this pious creativity and innovative beginning became dangerous as the Islamic Empire splintered and the caliph became the captive of his mercenary troops. To the secular interest of rival sultans and armies, the ulema could not counterpose the institutional power of any priestly hierarchy or established church. To save the spirit of the law, the ulema safeguarded its letter. By the tenth century, the ulema closed the "gate to individual interpretation" of the Sharia.

A living community, however, could scarcely abide by such a decision. The rulers continued as they had almost from the first, to develop administrative law (encompassing the entire realm of politics, jurisprudence, and government) as well as criminal, civil, and commercial law apart from Sharia law. The people, in turn, frequently sought to avoid the law courts of sultans and ulema by resorting to private vengeance or the arbitration of tribal chiefs and saintly men. If nothing else would help, they attempted to secure justice through nepotism, bribery, personal influence, and casuistry, or to restore it through rebellion.

In such asundering of the values and behavior of the various components of Islamic society lay the seeds of destruction. I have already discussed the creative defense of folk Islam against such moral and political division (cf. p. 59). In their search for certainty in this highly uncertain environment, sultans and ulema discovered that, however much at odds their final aims, they also needed each other.

The sultans recognized that the rule of naked force is the least secure of all authority. They required an ideological justification for their power, consonant with the pre-Islamic folk insistence upon the unity of politics and religion, even though they refused to accept the sharing of sovereignty implicit in this folk tradition. The ulema also could not countenance the unorthodox re'igio-political concepts championed by folk Islam. The ulema became the ideologists of the state, for they could not deny legitimacy to the realities of the Islamic history lest they imply that the Community of Believers has fallen away from the sacred law, and hence that the Community's judicial and religious activities were void (Gibb and Bowen 1950 : 26). "The concessions made by us are not spontaneous," said Abu Hamid al-Ghazali, a prominent medieval Muslim theologian, "but necessity makes lawful what is forbidden . . . . We should like to ask which is to be preferred, anarchy and the stoppage of social life for lack of a properly constituted authority, or acknowledgement of the existing power, whatever it be ? Of these two alternatives, the jurist cannot but choose the latter." In this way, the doctrine of the necessary unity of faith and politics, which justified rebellion of folk Islam, also became the justification employed by the ulema for demanding obedience to kings.

Though it would appear an unrewarding division of labor for the ulema to uphold one kind of norm while the powerful conformed to a different kind of practice, the role of the ulema was by no means without profit to the latter. For the role and doctrines of the ulema reflected and served well certain fundamental social interests. The minority of the ulema who counted politically—the muftis appointed by the sultan to issue formal interpretations of the Sharia, the Kadis who not only pronounced legal judgement but usually also supervised urban or provincial administration, and the ulema who acted as advisors to the sultans—almost invariably came from the most prominent families of the town, city or empire (Watt 1961). Almost all education was in their hands; almost all officials were educated by them. In the Ottoman Empire, their occupation became increasingly, though not exclusively, hereditary, like most other crafts (Coleman 1965). They also became tax-exempt. Thus "we can picture the bureaucrat" in the Muslim world, no less than in China "as a scholar-gentleman, with his roots in society, sensitive to the varied complexities of individual, social and family situations, and adapting the law and his own behavior to fit them, accommodating himself to state power...but checking it simply by being what he was" (Nivison and Wright 1959: 17).

The ulema's role in the service of the sultan was not without benefit to the rest of the community, for their ideology had a double-edged character. By supporting all existing authority—that of the successful usurper no less than the dynastic heir—the ulema were able to safeguard not only their own position, but also prevent both the ruler and community from quite forgetting the ideal code of conduct. By constantly reiterating that code, they maintained an implicit criticism of actual authority. By occupying many of the subsidiary positions of power, these ulema were able to modify the exercise of sultanic authority. They could filter or entangle royal commands through a web entwining the social, economic and legal interests represented or mediated by the ulema. A number of the more pious ulema refused to serve the government in any capacity. Their role in the Islamic system is discussed later on in this chapter.

Another autonomous set of tensions and balances existed in Islam to bind the entire society through conflict no less than through collaboration. Although kinship was Islam's most solid and enduring tie, relatives and kindred families and tribes often fought each other until menaced by a common enemy. Tribal blood ties were not immutable. Defeated, decimated, or dependent tribes were sometimes given the option of becoming clients of other tribes, and ultimately merging with them. Individuals were sometimes also given this privilege (Smith 1903). Almost all villages, tribes, and families in South-West Asia were, and often still are, divided into rival factions. These factions, cutting across class and status lines, acted as rival networks for marshalling influence and protection and for undermining the influence of others. They were, in a sense, the secular equivalent of the religious brotherhoods, providing for collaboration among individuals not related by consanguinity. The resulting alliances were often fickle and hence there was much political instability, but the very system that produced conflict also produced means for new collaborative combinations. Even when tribes were pacified or their chiefs granted bribes, individuals readily continued to conspire to power. In a society, divided by lines of blood, factionalism provided an important solvent, freeing men for collaboration regardless of kinship ties.

There were three groups whose members were, by their very nature, not firmly tied to the network of balanced tensions that in reality constituted Islam. Since it assumed that Allah's final truth had been fully revealed, the Islamic community found it difficult to make room for intellectuals bent on a search for truth. The recruitment of standing mercenary or slave armies to protect sultans against their Islamic rivals or Islamic subjects created elements of preponderant force difficult to match elsewhere in Islamic society. (Originally, the entire Muslim community had been expected to supply armed men for wars that were holy "jihad" because they were exclusively directed against non-Muslims.) Although the continual generation of saintly men must have been desired by the Prophet of Islam's original vision, his successors often found saints difficult to bear.

By their less fettered existence, all three—intellectuals, saints, and soldiers—often clearly revealed and challenged the limits of the Islamic system. During most of Islam's history, the saints and soldiers who raised Islam's spirit and power seemed also to be the principle threats to the survival of the system. The saints by their extreme, sometimes even heretical piety, endangered the system of balanced tensions that in fact held the Muslim community together; the soldiers threatened it by their exceedingly secular and unilateral concern for power. The pious and the men of arms helped, as we shall see, to bring about the decay of the traditional Islamic system. It was the intellectuals, however, who ultimately succeeded in destroying it.

Throughout Islamic history, some of the most pious Muslims refused to accept public office. They did not see how justice could triumph when those who knew the Sharia attempted to reconcile it with their loyalty to the sultan, family, and faction. Sometimes such saintly ulema or mystics were imprisoned or killed for their conscientious objections. When they publicly asserted the supremacy of absolute truth or the absolute good, they threatened the community by which the Islamic community lived.

The military found it easier than any other group in Islam to make its master; it made and unmade sultans. Because the army was usually recruited among slaves or mercenaries, and hence alien to the population among whom it was stationed, the soldiery commonly did not hesitate to extort a high price for its presence. It ravaged and wasted the community's resources in almost perennial warfare among Islamic military commanders. By possessing a preponderant power that could only imperfectly and infrequently be checked by other elements of the Islamic system, the military made it more difficult for the balanced tensions of Islam to remain in creative and renovating motion. By its overbearing weight, the army gradually made the Islamic system more static. In this way, and by its pre-emptive sapping of the region's material resources, it helped to bring about the decay of Islam (Watt 1961).

That decay was slowed, however, by the fact that even this most powerful and detached force was vulnerable to the operations of the Islamic pattern of action and mode of behavior. The army might have assured its supremacy, had it been able to convert itself into a stable, exclusive military caste. But it could not muster the strength, either through brute force or institutional transformation, entirely to put an end to social and political mobility in Islam. The army's own ranks frequently splintered, reflecting personal, factional, tribal, and religious conflicts. Army

regimes at times succumbed to the attacks of rival armies organized by other autonomous groups in the realm—the tribes and the
religious brotherhoods. In addition, the army could be infiltrated.
The Ottoman army had at first been composed of kidnapped or
recruited Christian children converted into Muslims and bound
to service as the sultan's personal property. By the seventeenth
century, this Janisary army became essentially a guild that, like
other crafts, had its particular rituals and saints and gained its
membership through inheritance or co-option.

But an army that had entirely adapted its outlook and organization, whether in a spirit of exploitation or integration to the
style of the Islamic system, was unprepared for an enemy whose
strength was derived from an entirely different style of life. Most
Muslim armies in Southwest and Central Asia were defeated by
modern Western "imperialists." A few Muslim rulers, among
them the rulers of the Ottoman Empire, sought refuge in copying
the enemies' modern weaponry and methods of training. They
discovered too late that these novel methods depended for their
effectiveness upon the development of new men and new socio-
cultural network of relationships, and that they had, therefore,
embarked on a course that could undermine the very system they
sought to save.

The intellectuals held the most precarious position in traditional
Islam. The educated men who accepted life as it was had ample
opportunity to serve the system as bureaucrat or one of the ulema.
But the independent intellectual, searching for truth rather than
believing it to have been already revealed with finality, was rare.
The essential spirit of Muslim culture, reinforced by rote and
political tyranny, discouraged their growth. Philosophers who
expressed their novel ideas and interpretations in deliberately
esoteric style survived, but, like Avicenna (Ibn Sina) and Aver-
roes (Ibn Rushd), at the price of being almost unread by his own
community. Philosophers who spoke plainly often suffered
physical harm; some like Suhrawardi (died 1191 A.H.) were
executed.

Certainly, the ulema and sultans were right in believing that
granting freedom to individual reason would jeopardize all other
established Islamic relationships. It was, indeed, the emergence

of a significant number of individuals claiming freedom for themselves in thought, technology, science, and society that ushered in the modern age and the destruction of the traditional Islamic system of prescriptions.

The traditional Islam bound the orthodox and heretic, the scholastic and mystic, the ruler and people in a single connected system of roles, values, orientations, and patterns of behavior. The combinations possible within that system were varied and unstable, but the system itself left play for all these uncertainties within rigidly defined patterns. It was a system in constant motion, like a prayer wheel, yet always anchored in the same place. Islam could provide all participants with a universal language of terms and symbols, just as the language of nationalism and social welfare had become the common tongue of the Asian and European, the capitalist and communist today. This common language reflected, however, not so much a common faith as a common fate. It was the language of all who accepted, exploited, enjoyed, justified, or rebelled against the limits within which life had to be lived. Whatever one's attitude, none could escape the terms of the encounter.

To describe Islam in this fashion, however, is to pay a price. In order to clarify the interaction of groups, interests, and beliefs, and show how opposing poles were bound in tension to each other, I have been indifferent to the historical direction and variegated complexion which Islamic society has taken in different periods, to its religious depth, and to the rich flowering of cultural achievement it once produced. The neglect of that cultural achievement is unfolding an injustice that cannot be remedied here, for my concern with the Islamic past is only with the problems it poses for the changing present—the focus of this thesis. Even so, the historical direction of the Islamic community that led to the present must be briefly indicated.

Long before the renaissance of Western Europe, Islam showed great flashes of creativity, critical reason, and vigor. Between the ninth and thirteenth centuries, one may at times find Muslim rulers encouraging the translation and discussion of Greek philosophy. A number of philosophers and historians wrote of themselves as individual human beings and analysed the actual processes of their society. Literature and science showed remarkable accomplishments. Merchants for a time plied a cosmopolitan trade unhindered by Islamic rules against banking. Ismai'ili heretics were accused of teaching that laws were merely enacted to hold down the masses and to maintain the worldly interests of those who rule (Lewis 1940-93). Farm workers turned religion into an ideological weapon against landlords. In what is probably one of the first examples of the use of the "sit down" (given the Muslim posture of prayer), a land owner complained in the late ninth century that the fifty prayers a day ordered by an imaginative Karmatian preacher interfered with the work of his laborers (Lewis 1940 : 92). The Karmatian preached the sharing of all property, but may have cared little about praying. Their sect won followers in large parts of Iraq, Syria, and Saudi Arabia between the ninth and eleventh centuries. Revolutions of laborers, artisans and peasants continued into the eleventh century. Yet by the end of the thirteenth century, Islam had remained resilient enough to defeat the Christian Crusaders, and attractive enough to convert the Turkish invaders into Muslims.

Unlike Western Europe, there was to be no renaissance or reformation. Islam continued to give birth to new empires, including by the sixteenth century the Ottoman Empire, the largest and most enduring among them, but the tug of war among the same forces continued, and the cast of characters did not change. The moral inspiration of Islam was never transformed into institutional power sufficient to sustain political authority permanently, yet also to limit its sway. The interplay of opposing interests among autonomous groupings in Islam never entered a lawful and public arena in which conflicts might find lasting reconciliation.

Instead, the Islamic system's characteristic mechanisms for constant renewal began to warp not long after the establishment of the Ottoman Empire, and sooner or later in other Muslim states. In an area of scarce resources, the predominance of the military had been achieved at the expense of the merchant and peasant. That imbalance was reinforced and became petrified as Islamic military and commercial expansion was foiled by Europe's growing power and greater trade with America and India, and the army could only strengthen itself by exploiting its own rulers and people.

The continued reiteration of the orthodox vision in the face of a corrupted reality finally discouraged creativity. It became impossible to use an orthodox vocabulary to speak clearly and honestly on current issues without hypocrisy or creating a false illusion. The persisting superiority of secular political institutions; the evermore characteristic ties of blood between ulema, who constituted the community's principal intellectual and moral leadership, and the politically and economically prominent families; and the lack of resources (both intellectual-human and physical) for altering a style of life based on perennial scarcity encouraged a man's spirit of acquiescence. Muslims became convinced that a man's heart mattered more than his behavior, eternity more than history. Even folk Islam turned its discontent inward and sought a better world through mysticism or dissipated its inner frustration through innocent exercises akin to those of the holy-rollers of American Protestantism. Its occasional rebellions confined themselves to protest against sultans who violated vested interests or established customs. The various Islamic brotherhoods seldom raised any longer the larger issue of social justice and morality.

As a result, the new emphasis on acquiescence strengthened Islam's endurance even while the checks and balances and the vitality of the Islamic system were deteriorating. Islamic society thus lingered basically unchanged until the late nineteenth century, and was therefore especially unprepared to meet the challenges of modernism.

REFORM AND SECULARIZATION

CHAPTER SIX

REFORM AND SECULARIZATION

MY CONCERN IN this portion of the dissertation is not *a priori* with Islam or any established ideology, but with how man must strike stable cultural roots amid the Muslim's permanently continuing transformation. Unlike some anthropologists, such as Malinowski (1945); Mair (1963); Wilson and Wilson (1945); and other functionalists, who would suggest merely adjusting to social change, my position is that it is better and easier to transform all aspects of society deliberately and quickly than be burdened continually with partial change. I am persuaded that remnants of the past tend "to reinstate the rest, and so continually act as a drag on the establishment of new habits....While it is dreadfully difficult to graft one foreign habit on a set of old habits, it is much easier and highly exhilarating to learn a whole new set of habits, each reinforcing the other as one moves...with as little reminder of the past as possible to slow down the learning, or make that learning incomplete and maladaptive" (Mead 1956:447 and 451). Incipient Muslim leaders who would establish the conditions in which Islamic systems can be innovative and self-generating, prosperous and self-sufficient, are, however, still scarce. Nasser and Bourguiba are only compromised converts to such radical transformation; Ataturk was one of the first.

Nevertheless, a new kind of society and cultural patterns are emerging among Muslims and with it the need to make new choices. Most Western scholars believe, this is a question that must involve the reformation of Islam. In fact, the great change proceeding apace in the Muslim world is not the deliberate reformation of Islam as a religious system but the transformation of Muslims as individuals and as members of a new society.

Choices will not come easily. The searching, detached, yet concerned intellectual is still a new and rare individual in the Muslim society. The great majority of "politically active" individuals desire the fruits of modernization, but few understand the methods or appreciate the cost of producing such a harvest. In some Muslim societies, this contrast between reach and grasp also characterizes the ruling elites. Yet in each country, one can already point to individuals and small groups (and in the Muslim world, the minority invariably rules), who are intent upon becoming organizers rather than victims of social change, and who are (understandably) concerned about political means and ends. The new leaders in the Muslim sphere cannot build upon inherited philosophy, customs, or institutions; nor is there any consensus on how to alter the legacy of Islamic tradition. Commitment to various ideologies thus usually takes the place of inherited, inner-directed certainty, both as the frame of analysis and as the inspiration for concerted action. Thus will be realized a total commitment to cultural transformation. Such is indeed the case of Turkey, as discussed earlier and which will be discussed in the following chapters with particular reference to secularization and a shift from a prescriptive to principial ideology.

Islamic history, from the perspective of the ulema, is the history of a community in process of realizing a divinely ordained pattern of society (Smith 1946; Gibb 1947). To pursue righteousness, however, means resolving the conflict of existence or, at least, learning how to live with them with dignity, patience, and compassion. As I have already mentioned, this was not infeasible during those centuries when Muslims had few new problems to solve, or else allowed practice to sanctify submission not only to Allah, but also to authoritarianism and community consensus. The practices thus ordained, however, belong to the pre-scientific, pre-industrial, pre-nationalistic age. The principles belong to the tenth century, when the ulema set the limits to the debate of basic questions. Although H.A.R. Gibb argues that "the future of Islam rests where it has rested in the past—on the insight of the orthodox leaders and their capacity to resolve the new tensions as they arise by a positive doctrine," he acknowledges that "in the attitude and outlook of the ulema and their followers there is a disturbing weakness. They are losing touch with the thought of the age. Their arguments, however just, fail to carry conviction because they are expressed in thought-forms which arouse no response in the minds of educated men. Even the very language which they generally use has an antiquarian flavor that strikes curiously upon the ear and eye and strengthens the feeling that they have no message for today. Above all, their public pronouncements display a rigid formalism and reliance upon authority which, as the modernists see truly, are but feeble weapons . . . ." (Gibb 1947:122-123).

The reformist ulema are trying to respond to the challenge of Western culture at a time when orthodox Islam has already lost its fervor, influence, and clarity. "In accord with God's command...Muslim society once erected a great civilization; but now this is seen as being attacked, without and within, and perhaps superseded, by a new power based on God's ordinance...a new society more successful, and perhaps in some aspects even more attractive. Islamic backwardness implies that something has gone wrong not only with the Muslim's own development but with the governance of the universe. . . . The challenge is no longer simply that the (Islamic) dream is unrealized. The new challenge...is in the fear of the recognition that the dream may be invalid, (that) even if implemented, (it) would...be too weak in the world of today" (Smith 1946:111-112).

The attempt of the ulema to reform Islam has met with difficulties. Like their predecessors in the first centuries of Islam, they acknowledge the usefulness of reason, provided that it is employed in the service of dogma. Only the reformist ulema go that far.

Others continue to say, "Islam is not our property for us to offer it to others, with alterations suitable to the requirements of the market" (Maudoodi 1967:115). Jamal-ad-Din al-Afghani and Mohammad Abduh, among the greatest thinkers of reformist Islam, were prepared near the turn of the century to accept the scientific theories of the nineteenth century. They departed far enough from orthodox Islam to welcome the idea that laws and regulations control the universe of nature. They objected to the science's mechanistic concepts of causation and in their own works reassured Muslims that Allah was the author of these scientific laws. They felt that they were simply acknowledging that the world had become more comprehensible, while preserving their own religion since it now appeared that the whole universe was Islamic in character: everything, even the stars, must submit to the laws of Allah.

Rereading the Koran they discovered a verse that has since been quoted more often by Muslim reformers, both secular and religious, than parhaps any other commanding initiative and self-help: "Verily, Allah changes not what a people has until they change it for themselves" (Koran XIII:12). But this verse continues in quite a different vein, and the reformers do not quote its remainder: "And Allah wishes evil to people there is no averting it, nor have they a protector beside Him." Careful reinterpretation of the Koran also seemed to suggest to the reformers of Islam that the most modern discoveries had long been foreshadowed in it. The verse, "He has created you by steps," for example, was thought to anticipate the theory of evolution: "What ails you that ye hope not for something serious from Allah, when he has created you by steps?" (Koran LXXI:12-13).

The Koranic permission to marry four women, but to treat them impartially, was interpreted by some reformists to mean the contrary of what had already been assumed. Since no man can treat four women with equal justice, the Koran, in fact, prescribes monogamy. Unfortunately, the reinterpretation frequently sounded more incredible to modern ears than the original gloss. Even so, one cannot help feeling that the reformers were driven more by reason than by faith. Mohammad Abduh, for example, was capable of writing, "If the reformers appeal directly to a morality or to a wisdom deprived of all religious character, he will have to build a new edifice for which there is neither material nor labor. But if religion is able to raise the level of morality...if the adepts of this religion are very attached to it, if finally one has less difficulty in bringing them back to this religion than in creating something new of which they are not clearly conscious, why not have recourse to the religion, and why seek other less effective means" (Abduh 1957:177).

More serious is the fact that since Jamal-ad-Din (died 1897) and Mohammed Abduh (died 1905), there have been almost no reformist ulema or popularizers of equal stature or influence anywhere in the Islamic world. In the Arab world, the successors of these two reformers became increasingly divided among conservatives, extremists, and radicals (Smith 1946:115-156; Khalid 1953). In Muslim India, and now Pakistan, the poetic philosophy of Mohammed Iqbal (1876-1938), reconstructing Sufism rather than Orthodox Islam along modern lines, has remained an inspiration to many, but a practical guide to very few. His most significant work is *The Reconstruction of Religious Thought in Islam*, 1934. Among the most interesting discussions of Iqbal are those of C.W. Smith, *Modern Islam in India;* and H.A.R. Gibb, *Modern Trends in Islam*.

The reformist ulema have not altogether won the battle even among their own group. Education, as long as it is under the control of the ulema, is still bound up with authoritarianism, providing only already known solutions to already formulated problems. Where education is under secular control, as in the case of Turkey (see Chapter Nine), Islam is either neglected or enlisted in the service of the state. Where the influence of the ulema lingers, religion and science are still at odds, since even reformist Islam countenances the revealed truth. Indeed, the ulema have no idea how great the issue really is since none of them have studied any of the major sciences of the twentieth century. However, there is a small but potentially significant minority that is indeed the exception to this rule. As the Muslim demand for social and physical sciences increases, most Muslim intellectuals will be increasingly drawn to its pursuit. One fears (but is relieved) that this will be done at the cost of ignoring a reformist Islam which has so far failed to relate itself to the modern techno-scientific world.

Like orthodox Islam, its offshoot is directly concerned with the social and economic problems of daily existence (see the Koran, Sura II, verses 278-285 for a characteristic example of Mohammed's interests in the economic details of daily life). It formulates its attitude with awareness, though seldom with a thorough understanding, of capitalist, socialist, and communist alternatives. Reformist Islam proposes its system as a middle road between communism and capitalism, without the excesses of either. Its theories appear in a number of different forms (Lerner 1959). The case of Nasser and Egypt; Sukarno and Indonesia; Pakistan and Ayub Khan provide other substantive illustrations.

One school quotes the Koran to show that while private property, unequal social status, and the accumulation, though not the hoarding, of wealth are justified (Koran VI:20), and none are to be regarded as highly as the mercy of Allah (Koran XLIII: 32). Wealth must be spent with neither extravagance nor waste, and above all, with compassion for those in need (Koran IX:34; XVII:29; LXX:24-25; LVII:7). Usury (interest in any amount) is forbidden (Koran II:275-280). This school tends at times to assume a passive, defensive stand, asserting that since Islam already includes the best of other economic systems, there is no need to tamper with it; that, in fact, communism, socialism and capitalism must be fought as perversions of ideal Islam. It supports the inherited system of landowning, whether it is based on the traditional pattern of the political and economic power of big landlords, on the fragmentation of lands brought about by the strict application of Islamic inheritance laws, or on lands divided only in usufruct under the same laws and leaving hundreds of heirs for each lot with little opportunity for enterprising management. It relies on philanthropy and the *zakat* (a religious levy of about 2.5 per cent on annual revenues in lieu of taxes for social welfare). In short, reformist Islam sometimes substitutes religious piety for economic reform.

There are times when reformist Islam appears to be a dynamic program for the modern welfare state. Consider a Ramadan sermon on "Islam and communism": "Islam guaranteed the working man's living conditions before communism ever existed on earth....Islam, however, not only encourages the people to demand and struggle for their rights, but even prescribes in its holy verses that those who give up their natural rights expose themselves to severe chastisement. . . . Islam has given to the poor liens both on capital and on the rich. It has guaranteed to all social classes equity in the field of life. Islam protects the whole of the people from hunger and nakedness. Islam has condemned the monopoly of wealth in the hands of any group to the prejudice of others. Islam has recommended liveliness and hard work and prescribed that no harvest can be obtained without tilling, no wealth without toil" (Abdallah 1951). When it speaks in such a fashion, one concludes that reformist Islam has severed all connection with orthodoxy except that of language.

Orthodox Islam looks upon the universe as a sacred unity of man and nature, reality and idea, cousciousness and existence. Reformist Islam perceives a conflict between man and uncontrolled nature, secular reality and religious truth, man's humanity and the increasing atomization of his social relations. It hopes to recapture Islam's lost unity by a philosophic and hypothetical reconstruction of revealed truth. By shifting the emphasis from the letter to the spirit of the Koran, it seeks to convert Islam into a set of broad formulas that make the existing social relations emotionally comfortable, and provides for emotional ease. At worst, reformist Islam sometimes gives the impression of being at work to save not the world of men, but itself (Smith 1945:84). Reformist Islam's present formulations lack one important attribute of a living religion—immediacy of assent. Reformists for all their explaining and justifying, cannot yet offer a restatement of Islam that strikes a balance between "the broad and deep currents of a people's psychology and the inescapable forces of social evolution (Gibb 1955:113).

The reformist ulema are unlikely to succeed. From the Prophet Mohammed onward, the orthodox interpreters of Islam have made themselves acceptable to the community by allying themselves with existing social institutions and so enlarging the consensus of belief. Indeed, the special strength of Islam's orthodox and even its heretics has always been, that for them all things— sacred, secular, legal, ethical, intellectual, emotional, political, social, economic—are and ought to be related. Today, social institutions are in conflict and the consensus is broken. From an Islamic perspective, the failure of the reformist ulema is that they have managed no better than secular reformers, such as Ataturk, in putting the pieces together again toward a productive, self-sufficient, and reasonable society.

The failure of the ulema to produce a new intellectual synthesis stems in part from an endemic weakness of traditional Islam. Analytical philosophy has always seemed impious to the orthodox Muslims—a sacreligious and ultimately doomed effort to lay bare Allah's essence, meaning, and purpose. In the relatively static world of the past, this weakness in philosophical inquiry made Islam more tolerant than Christianity of theological differences within, and often even outside the Muslim world, and thereby contributed to the stability and, within limits, the flexibility of the community. In the search for Allah, practice counted for more than reason. Now that practices, theories, and faiths are in conflict in Islamic systems, the ulema, even when they consent to use reason, can only contribute additional opinions to the broken consensus.

By continuing to be tolerent as long as Islamic dogma is not explicitly denied, the largest proportion of the ulema in Islam are likely to acquiesce, as they always have, in the policies of their secular rulers, but this time with uprooting, dislocation and irreversible consequences.

As the ulema stand aside, whether by choice or necessity, the very center of orthodox Islam—Sharia law is slipping beyond the control of its guardians. Majid Khadduri has outlined the initial steps leading toward the secularization of Islamic law. First, the adoption of Western legal rules and principles which are either not adequately covered by the Sharia or not mentioned at all by the Sharia; second, the adoption of Western law which is, in principle, in conformity with the Sharia, but is not dealt with in such detail as would fit the conditions of modern life as influenced by the West...third, the adoption of Western law which may take the place of certain Sharia rules that have become obsolete; fourth, the separation of the devotional and religious provisions of the Sharia from those regulating daily life (Khadduri 1956: 232).

The spirit with which secular law is being assimilated is even more significant than its structural form. Khadduri attributes the success of one of the leading architects of secular law, Abd al-Rassaq al-Sanhur—the principle author of recent Egyptian, Syrian, and Iraqi civil codes—to the fact that al-Sanhuri "wisely abstained from discussing controversial issues that might have brought him into conflict with the ulema and interrupted his work." He proceeded "without going into a theoretical discussion on how the Sharia generally should be modernized, or even trying to give a rationale to his scheme...." (Khadduri 1956:232). His is a revolutionary work which is conservative in intent and style. He dares to revise revealed and divine law by individual judgement, but he seeks to maintain respect for law by artfully sustaining at least the verisimilitude of historical continuity.

By avoiding a discussion of principles, however, the conservative modernists have not only succeeded in quietly imposing their own revisions, but have failed to set clear limits to the revolution they began. In a community originally founded to perpetuate a revealed code of conduct as defined by the Sharia, the latter has by now ceased to be the primary source of ethics, and insofar as its rules survive in modern laws, it has ceased to be either divine or final. Even the last and strongest fortress of the original code—family law—has already yielded as will be discussed later on. By now, there are few Muslim countries in which the laws bearing on polygyny, divorce, child-marriage, private religious endowment (*waqf*), and inheritance have not been decisively altered.

Once everyone was free to make judgement, it was clear that the Sharia would have to give way. There was no longer a single highway into the future. The Turks did not bother to retain any part of the Sharia. In 1959, at a congress of Arab lawyers for studying the unification of civil codes in Arab countries, the delegates at times differed so sharply among themselves that the Beirut police were called in to restore order (reported in *New York Times, Times,* September 7, 1959). Even at the Arab citadel of Sharia traditlonalism, al-Azhar University in Cairo, Shaikh Khallaf could write: "...the goal of the law is only the welfare of men. There is the law of God" (Nolte 1958:306).

Thus divine law yields to man-made law, which is enacted not for a community of believers but for nations that neglect the traditional Islamic distinction among subjects on the basis of creed. At that point, the old relationship between the sacred and the secular, the expedient and the metaphysical, is forever shattered and must be built anew. Without the Sharia, Islam possesses an all-powerful Allah without adequate guidance concerning his will, a holy book without agreed upon interpretations, a religious emotion without clear ethical and social consequences, and authority in the community without traditional legitimacy.

Those who would reform Islam strictly within the framework of the past lost their first and decisive battle when they themselves amended the past, and thus opened the door to innovation. By now, enough change has taken place so that even the ulema no longer agree on what constitutes an Islamic state. Islam, never the single vision of the ulema, has by now almost as many faces (and many of these new) as there are Muslims. Today, any attempt to assert one interpretation of Islam, however hallowed by the past or sensitively reconstructed, as binding on all, cannot help but become merely a partisan effort. Insofar as Muslims who have broken with the consensus of kin and tradition still acknowledge each other as "Muslims," it is a common act of individual wills.

Certainly far more educated Muslims than Western orientalists have, proportionately, become indifferent to traditional Islam (Kritzeck 1959:320). Muslim leaders may still use, although with diminishing frequency, an Islamic vocabulary as the most widely understood and least controversial means of communication. When President Gamal Nasser of Egypt in December, 1958 decided to warn Iraq, whose secular-minded leadership shares with him common origins and goals, that is, "neutralism" was too far toward the Sino-Soviet bloc, he declared that their attitude was contrary to the spirit of Islam. When references to Islam did not change Iraq's policy, Nasser did not, however, deem it useful to enlarge on this theme. A real debate could only be supported on modern ideological grounds. But Islam, not as a polity, but as a unique and ordained pattern for politics, economics, and society at large is no longer practiced anywhere in the Muslim world, except in portions of the Arabian Peninsula. Even here, the substance, if not the form, is increasingly being diluted.

The division among Muslims has gone so far that even those who still employ an Islamic vocabulary often can no longer understand each other. The delegates who arrived at the Islamic Colloquium at Lahore, West Pakistan, in December, 1957, found a leaflet in their mail which read: "Dear Delegates to the Islamic Colloquium.... You are already aware that this is an Islamic country and our constitution is based on the Holy Quran and Sunna. Kindly therefore take care not to inquire about the feelings of the Muslims of this Islamic country, in any way, by saying things against Islam, its history, its culture, and its laws."

On the following day, the then President of Pakistan, General Iskander Mirza, in welcoming the delegates, declared: "Islam is too dynamic and too eternal to be imprisoned in the requirements of a passing age. As the intellect of man develops into new dimensions with the discoveries of new avenues of knowledge and science, his understanding of life and religion is bound to grow in similar proportions....It is an irony of history that, while rejecting the institutions of organized priesthood, Islam has often fallen into the hands of priests....On the one hand, the Mullah (another term to designate one of the ulema) has woven into Islam a crazy network of fantasy and fanaticism. On the other, he has often tried to use it as an elastic cloak for political power and expediencies." Since then, I might add that General Mirza has been ousted from the Presidency by another general (Ayub Khan) who thought him not radical enough in dealing with Pakistan's problem and who abolished the constitution that had made Pakistan at the time the only formally designated "Islamic Republic" in Asia.

For the Muslims who are taking the leading roles in the Islamic national-cultural systems, the battle has moved from the realm of religion to the realm of politics. "Relief of distress is sought not in a revision of doctrine but in a redressing of history" (Smith 1966:111). Kenneth Cragg writes in a similar vein: "Islam has always believed that the individual, not the community, is the source of 'heresy.' It is a corollary of this that social change, not intellectual enterprise, must be the proper origin of religious redefinition" (1955:160). No one attacks Islam. Ataturk, the most far-reaching of the secularists, did not challenge the Islamic faith, nor did any of the political leaders that came after him (Berkes 1964).

There was no need, perhaps, to challenge it. Reformist Islam opened the sluice gate and was swamped by the deluge. Traditional Islam still has many adherents among the peasant majority and not a few urbanites. This is elaborated in the chapter dealing with secular education and modernization in Turkey. No political leader is likely to challenge and thus outrage their sensibilities by deliberately speaking ill of Islam. Almost all of them concentrate instead on eliminating particular Islamic institutions and customs that stand in the way of modernization. Their methods are many: financing secular schools (as in the case of Turkey) and neglecting Koranic-religious schools, favoring men with secular outlook in government appointments, enlarging opportunities for women, making no allowance for easier working hours during the fasting month of Ramadan (as in the case of Tunisia), generally rewarding new types of knowledge, values, and modes of behavior. Even changes in clothing have consequences for Islam. When in 1925 Ataturk compelled the Turks to adopt the Western hat in place of the traditional fez, he made prayer more difficult since a headgear is mandatory and the worshipper's head must bend over to touch the ground, and also made it harder to distinguish Muslims from non-Muslims. When traditional Islam reacts by transforming itself into a religio-political totalitarian theme, it can safely be challenged as a novel ideology rather than as a hallowed way of life. (See my conclusions stated in the last chapter.) There will still be battles but this particular war is over in the great majority of the Muslim states.

The secularization of political leadership turned out unexpectedly to be even easier in the Islamic sphere than in Western Europe, where the distinction between the things of Caesar and those of God did not prevent Christians from fighting each other long and fiercely. The secularization of the masses remains the great unfinished business in the Muslim world. Perhaps the speed of secularization among the decision-makers should not have been unexpected. Few Muslim rulers in history have made it the main business of the state, as the Koran had intended, to enforce Allah's eternal laws.

Administrative, criminal, civil and commercial laws had almost from the beginning of the Islamic community been separated from the domain of the Sharia, though this separation was not formally and explicitly codified until the nineteenth century. Islam had also early reconciled itself to the separation between religion and the conduct of the state in foreign affairs, once it acquiesced in the peaceful coexistence of orthodox Islamic states with Christian and heterodox Islamic nations. The "principle of the peaceful relationship among nations of different religions...perhaps the most revolutionary in Islamic legal theory, was for the first time embodied in a treaty signed in 1535 between Francis I of France and Sulayman the Magnificent, sultan of the Ottoman Empire" (Khadduri 1959:51; 1955). Most Muslims have therefore long been accustomed to obey secular-minded rulers, or to avoid the rule of sultans and ulema by frequently resorting to private vengeance, arbitration by tribal chiefs, and the subversion of justice through nepotism, bribery, personal influence, and casuistry.

The ulema have always been steadfast but unheroic. Mohammed Abduh, for example, the founder of the Egyptian Islamic reform movement, said in 1905, when Egypt was still under British occupation, "but the matter of the government and the governed I abandoned to the decision of fate, and to the hand thereafter to arrange" (Adams 1933:63-64). As a result, Egypt's largest nationalist party, then led by Mustapha Kamil, went a separate way (Gibb and Bowen 1955:1:72). Many mosques have endowments, but there is no central church-like control over large properties to give added strength to a defense of sacred institutions. And not only the frequency of heresies and the popularity of non-orthodox mystic orders, but the very autonomy of social structures and functions discussed in an earlier chapter suggest that the Islamic community of the past was more united in the style of its certainties than in their substance.

Yet even the end of certainty was eased by a number of historical factors. Few Muslims thoroughly understood the choices to be made between the traditional past and modern present since in fact they were ill-informed about either. Islam had fallen into political, economic, spiritual, and general cultural decay prior to the arrival of Western "imperialism." "The Kingdom and crowns that the Moslems have lost in the course of history," Pakistan's President Ayub Khan told his audience when he accepted an honorary doctorate of philosophy at Cairo University, "are far less important than the kingdom of the free and searching mind, which they lost in the process of intellectual stagnation" (reported in *New York Times*, November 11, 1960). It is also illuminating to witness the differentially successful efforts of Ottoman, Wahabi, and Sanusi reformers, each in their own way, to rescue their own society. As against such a way of life—the days of greatest Islamic unfolding had passed centuries earlier—modernity often offered immediate advantages. Certainly, the great majority of Muslims had neither liberty nor property to lose in the death of the past.

Men who were born in the twentieth century grew up in an Islamic society that had already begun to question its verities. They no longer faced the same conflicts of adjustment that confronted their fathers. In the constant invasion of the "barbarians"— Westerners—and the continual generation of the young, learning much about their world but little about their own heritage, there lie many opportunities for startling individual transformations in the midst of rapid socio-cultural change.

For Arabs probably more than for other Muslims, many Islamic memories remain precious for being also specifically Arab memories—perhaps the grandest Arab memories. Nonetheless, it has become easier for all Muslims to discover and admire what other so-called undeveloped areas of Asia, Latin America, and Africa are doing in changing their traditional way of life. Of the entire social and cultural inheritance of Islam, it is the force of consensus along with the unfeasibility of the unity of state and Islam (with few exceptions, of course) which has remained the strongest moral imperative in the Muslim world. These two features hold sway, in varying degrees over many through the compulsion of family or village opinion, reinforced by faith in the infallibility of the consensus (*ijma*) of the "charismatic Community of Believers" (Watt 1961). Increasingly, however, this insistence on the hallowed consensus is itself becoming a force for change as the pressure for conformity comes no longer from one's ancestors but from one's peers. Novel ideas can be accepted in the name of national unity and national ideology.

These new guides to conformity may now lead either toward responsible and productive freedom or away from it. In any event, the most actively concerned are aware that Muslims, like their neighbors, have many new alternatives before them. A discussion of the most predominatly chosen alternative—the revitalization of the past—will be included in my concluding remarks.

THE CONCEPT OF PROGRESS AND ISLAMIC
LAW

CHAPTER SEVEN

THE CONCEPT OF PROGRESS AND ISLAMIC LAW

SOUTH-WEST ASIA IS renowned for the oldest legal systems known in recorded history, and Islamic law, a part of its surviving cultural heritage, is one of the most prevalent legal systems of the world. Many of these systems had been exposed to foreign influences, but Islamic law has preserved its basic character. The greatest challenge in recent years has come from the West, under the impact of which Islamic law is bound to change. Perhaps it is too early to hazard a prediction; but there are signs which indicate that this impact may well mark a new milestone in the development of the Islamic legal system. The purpose of this chapter is to first illustrate the internal changes that have occurred in Islamic law which in turn have resulted in the development of the four major schools of Muslim law; and secondly, to discuss recent significant changes that have transpired in the structure of this legal system in regard to the family laws. Due to the unavailability of substantive data, changes in other spheres of the structure are not examined, but it should be obvious that parallel changes have taken place in the other dimensions of the structure of Islam. Thus, the focus will be on the processes of change and the forces operating to transform the law from a medieval to a modern legal order.

"All innovation is the work of the devil." These alleged words of the founder Prophet of Islam, Mohammed, do not merely reflect the innate conservatism and the deep-seated attachment to tradition that were so strong among the Arab peoples who formed the first adherents of the faith. They also express a principle that became a fundamental axiom of religious belief in Islamic communities everywhere—namely, that the code of conduct represented by the religious law, or Sharia, was fixed and final in its terms and that any modification would necessarily be a deviation from the one legitimate and valid standard.

Among Muslim peoples, therefore, it is what we may call the traditional or classical Islamic concept of law and its role in society that constitutes a most formidable obstacle to progress. Western jurisprudence has provided a number of different answers to the questions about the nature of law, finding its source variously, in the orders of a political superior in the framework of the judiciary, in the "silent anonymous forces" of evolving society, or in the very nature of the universe itself (Riesman 1954:440-466). For Islam, however, this same question admits of only one answer, which the religious faith itself supplies. Law is the command of Allah, and the acknowledged function of Muslim jurisprudence from the beginning was simply to discover the terms of that command (Hoebel 1965).

The religious code of conduct thus established was an all-embracing one in which every aspect of human relationships was regulated in meticulous detail. Furthermore, the law, having once achieved perfection of expression, was in principle, static and immutable, for Mohammed was the last prophet, and after his death in A.D. 632, there could be no further direct communication of the divine will to man. From then on, the religious law was to float above Muslim society as disembodied soul, representing the eternally valid ideal toward which man must aspire (Watt 1962; Coulson 1964).

In classical Islamic theory, therefore, law does not grow out of, or develop along with, an evolving society, as the case with the Western systems, but is imposed from above. In the Islamic concept, human thought unaided cannot discern the true values and standards of conduct; such knowledge can be attained only through divine revelation, and acts are good or evil exclusively because Allah has attributed this quality to them. Law, therefore, precedes and is not preceded by society; it controls and is not controlled by the society. Although in the Western systems the law is molded by society, in Islam exactly the converse is true. The religious law provides the comprehensive, divinely ordained and eternally valid master plan to which the structure of state and society must ideally conform.

Obviously, the clash between the dictates of the rigid and static religious law and any impetus for change that a society may experience poses for Islam a fundamental problem of principle. Some Muslim countries, such as Turkey, Tunisia, Soviet Central Asia, have sought the solution in a process that may be termed "legal modernism." It is in part the purpose of this chapter to appreciate in broad outline the nature of changes that have come about. I propose to focus my attention here upon one particular legal reform introduced in Tunisia in 1957: The outright prohibition of polygyny, which represented a complete break with the legal tradition of some thirteen centuries (Goode 1963:87-202). I have chosen this particular case not because polygyny is one of the most pressing problems in Islam—it is generally not so (Hourani 1954 and Daghestani 1953) but because first, it involves the status of the family, where the influence of the traditional religious law has always been stronger; second, it highlights various issues in legal reform that are so common to Muslim communities the world over; and finally, it is one of the most extreme and significant examples of the process of legal modernism, which may not radically alter the structure of Islamic society but also may affect the very nature of the Islamic religion itself. My approach to the subject is essentially historical, for it is only in the light of past tradition that the significance of legal modernism and its potential role in the future development of Islamic peoples may be properly assessed.

Traditional Muslim jurisprudence is an example of a legal

science almost totally divorced from historical considerations. Islamic orthodoxy views the elaboration of the law as a process of scholastic endeavor completely independent of and in isolation from considerations of time and place, and the work of individual jurists during the formative period is measured by the single standard of its intrinsic worth in the process of discovery of the divine command (Schacht 1964). Master architects were followed by builders who implemented the plans; successive generations of craftsmen made their own particular contributions to the fixtures, fittings, and interior decor, until the task completed; future jurists were simply to serve as passive caretakers of the eternal edifice. This elaboration of the system of Allah's commands lacks any true dimension of historical depth. Recent researches by scholars (Coulson 1964; Schacht 1964; Von Grunebaum 1955), however, have shown that the genesis of Islamic religious law lay in a complex process of historical growth intimately connected with current socio-cultural conditions, and extending over the first three centuries of Islam.

The first steps in Islamic jurisprudence were taken in the early years of the second century of the Muslim era, around A.D. 750, by scholars working in various centers, of which the most important were Kufa in Iraq and Medina in the Hijaz. For most scholar-jurists, the fundamental axiom of Islam—that of total submission to Allah, meant that all human relationships were subject to regulation by the divine command. Their aim, therefore, was to elaborate a system of law that would express, in terms of the rights of men and their obligations, the will of Allah for Muslim communities, a system to be called the Sharia. But for those loose fraternities of legal scholars, which I may call "the early schools of law," in this activity entailed nothing more than the assessment of existing legal practices in the light of the principles embodied in the Koran. The Koran does not contain a code of law in any sense. It sets out merely to reform, in a limited number of particulars, the existing customary law by precepts that often suggest rather than command; they are predominantly ethical in tone, and amount to about 100 verses in all. The Koranic legislation, in fact, amounts to little more than the preamble to a code of conduct for which succeeding generations were to supply the operative parts.

Accordingly, there was wide scope for the use of reason, or *ijtihad*, as it came to be called in the formulation of the doctrine. And it is not surprising that this freedom to speculate led to considerable divergence of doctrine among different localities (Kerr 1966). For outside the limited field covered by the Koranic precepts, the thought of the scholar was naturally influenced by the particular cultural conditions prevailing in their localities, and local customary practice was accepted as part of the ideal scheme of things unless some explicit principle of the Koran was flagrantly violated. Let me briefly take one outstanding example of such divergence.

The law of Medina held that every woman, minor or adult, could contract a marriage only through her guardian (for this purpose, a close male relative like the father or the paternal grandfather). If the guardian did not conclude the contract on her behalf, the marriage would be a nullity. Furthermore, the guardian possessed the power to give his ward in marriage regardless of her consent or lack of it, and again this law applied whether the female concerned was a minor or adult. These rules were natural enough in the traditionally tribal and patriarchal society of Medina, where inferior status of women and the tribal pride in marriage alliances combined to place power to contract a marriage in the hands of the male members of the society. But in Kufa, the rules were fundamentally different. There the adult women were completely free to contract marriage for themselves without the intervention of any guardian and could never be given in marriage without their free consent. These rules were conditioned in turn by the particular cultural climate of Kufa, where the cosmopolitan-urban atmosphere, resulting from the very mixed population of a new town in a predominantly Persian milieu, naturally allowed women greater freedom and higher social status. For the greater part of the eighth century, therefore, Islamic law was represented by a number of different legal systems in concert with their respective cultural settings, built around the basic precepts of the Koranic rules, systems designed to fit the varying conditions of the different cultural spheres.

The practical approach, however, was not to remain for long

unchallenged. The oppositions materialized in the form of a conservative group who sought to enlarge the area of law specifically
regulated by the divine command. They did so by appealing to
the authority of the Prophet of Islam. Such legal decision as the
Prophet himself had given, they argued, must be regarded as
divinely inspired, and it was these prophetic precedents, positive
manifestations of the divine will, rather than the custom of a
particular cultural locality that could form the only acceptable
supplement to the Koranic revelations. So formulated, the appeal
of this thesis was irresistible, and the zeal of its exponents resulted
in the discovery and collection of a great mass of reports and
alleged rulings of the Prophet, which were termed *hadith* and which
represented not what the Prophet actually did say or do but what
this group was convinced, in all good faith, that he would have
said or done in the circumstances envisaged. Prior to that time
(A.D. 900), all indications suggest the establishment in the early
schools of law had regarded the Prophet as a human interpreter
of the Koran because he was the closest in time and spirit to the
Koran, but nonetheless a human and therefore fallible interpreter
(Watt 1964:46). Members of the establishment, however, could
no longer maintain the validity of their own human reason in the
face of what was asserted by the doctrinnaire opposition group to
be divinely inspired conduct, and they reacted by gradually
expressing their own doctrines in the form of *hadith* from the
Prophet.

From this point onward, Muslim jurisprudence evolved a legal
theory that expressed to perfection the notion of Sharia law as a
divinely ordained system. This theory asserts that there are two
material sources of law and two only (Schacht 1964). The primary
source is, naturally enough, the very word of Allah himself as
expressed in the Koran, and the second source is the body of
precedents established by the Prophet and recorded in the *hadith*.
Known collectively as the *sunna* of the Prophet, these precedents
represent material, divine in its content, if not in its form, the function of which is to explain, interpret, and supplement the fundamental Koranic precepts. Questions that are not specifically
answered in these two sources and new problems and conditions
that may arise are to be solved and dealt with by a disciplined

form of reasoning, by analogy known as *qias* that is to say, by deducing from parallel cases regulated by the Koran and the Sunna the principles to be applied to these new cases. This theory therefore achieves a synthesis of the roles of divine revelation and human reason in law, but before it came to be generally accepted, the basic concept of principle involved produced further schools of law in addition to those that already existed.

The first systematic exposition of this novel theory of the sources of law was the work of the famous jurist al-Shafi'i, who died early in the third century of Islam. Initially, there was strong opposition to his thesis in the established schools of law in Kufa and Medina, which both continued to support far wider use of human reason in the formulation of the law than al-Shafi'i's insistence upon the restricted method of analogical deduction allowed. Accordingly, the immediate and convinced disciples of al-Shafi'i formed a group apart from the Shafi'i school, and on the basis of his teachings elaborated a body of doctrines that differed considerably from that recognized by the schools of Kufa and Medina. On the other hand, there were extremist elements who refused to accept the validity of any kind of human reason at all in law, rejected the use of analogical deduction, and purported to rely exclusively upon the Koran and the Sunna as sources of law (Coulson 1964). In the late third century of Islam, this group formed the Hanbali school, taking its name from the founder of the movement, Ahmad Bin Hanbal. Their particular jurisprudential principles are responsible for many distinctive and individual features of positive law that stand in sharp contrast to those of the other schools. One such feature calls for consideration here, as it is highly relevant to the question of polygyny.

Contract law in general, according to the views of the majority of Muslim jurists, consists of a series of individual and strictly regulated types of contract. Once a person enters into one of these defined contractual relationships, certain rights and obligations must result, and it is in general not permissible for the parties to modify or avoid these results by mutual agreement in the form of a stipulation in the contract.

As applied to contracts of marriage, this principle means that the marital relationship, the result of the contract, is defined by the law in terms of the rights and obligations that accrue to the husband and wife respectively. One of the rights that the law ascribes to the husband is the right to polygyny, the right to take additional wives up to the maximum of four concurrently. Should the parties agree by stipulation in the contract that the husband will not take a second wife during this marriage, they attempt to deny what the law regards as essential rights of the husband. This they cannot do. The stipulation is void and does not bind the husband (Levy 1957). If he breaks it and takes a second wife, the first wife has no remedy. This approach, which largely negates any concept of contractual freedom, does not arise from any dictates of the Koran. It is simply the result of the liberal *ijtihad* of the early jurists, based upon local practice and influenced strongly by the concepts of Roman Law current in the former provinces of the Roman Byzantine Empire. For the early Hanbali lawyers, such juristic speculation was, as I have already mentioned, devoid of any authority. Relying exclusively upon the Koran and *hadith* and in particular upon the Koranic text, "Muslims must honor this stipulation," they held that the courts must give effect to any stipulation that the parties to a contract might mutually agree upon, provided only that such stipulation did not involve anything expressly forbidden by the law and was not manifestly contrary to the institution of marriage that a man should have only one wife. If then, the husband makes an agreement not to take a second wife, Hanbali law regards this stipulation as enforceable, not in the sense that the husband will be prevented from marrying additional wives but in the sense that, if he does so, the first wife can claim a dissolution of her marriage.

In contrast to the Shafi'i and Hanbali schools, whose law was formally derived from the sources laid down in the legal theory, the early schools of Kufa and Medina had already developed a corpus of positive law before the legal theory was formulated. These two schools have become known as the Hanafi and Maliki schools respectively, taking these names from leading representative scholars and, although they eventually adopted al-Shafi'i's theory of the sources of law, they retained this pre-established body of positive law, and simply harmonized it, by devious means, with the dictates of the legal theory. For the Malikis and the Hanafis,

the legal theory was a formal and *post fact* rationalization of existing doctrine, and the result was that doctrines that had in fact
originated in particular local customs and individual juristic
reasoning came to be represented as expressions of the divine command. The same is true, as a matter of fact, of Shafi'i and
Hanbali law, for the purported prophetic precedents that were
their corner-stones were in reality largely expressions of local precedents and the views of particular scholars. For example, I
referred previously to the fact that Medinese law required every
woman to be given in marriage by her guardian, while the law of
Kufa allowed an adult woman to contract her own marriage
without the intervention of her guardian. Hanafi law preserved
the Kufa tradition and Maliki law, the Medinese tradition, and,
as the latter came to be expressed in the form of a Hadith from the
Prophet, it was taken over by the Shafi'i and Hanbali schools.
Accordingly, whenever the Hanafi schools prevail in Islam today,
as it does in Pakistan, the Indian subcontinent, an adult woman
had the capacity to conclude her own marriage contract (Goode
1963). But a woman has no such capacity where the Shafi'i school
prevails, as it does in South-East Asia—a distinction that has grown
from the particular localized socio-cultural circumstances obtaining in Kufa and Medina in the seventh century A.D. (Geertz
1960).

The final stage in the historical evolution of the classical Islamic
concept of law was perhaps the inevitable result of this idealistic
identification of every term of the law with the command of Allah
and the growing rigidity that such identification entailed. The
material sources of the divine revelation, the Koran and the
Sunna, were fixed and final in their form. There were obvious
limits to the exploitation of this material by way of interpretation
and analogical deduction, and by the beginning of the ninth
century, the belief had gained ground that this task had been
completed and that nothing further remained to be done (De
Santillan 1931). Perhaps the chief factor contributing to this
process of ossification was the development of the principle of
Ijma, the consensus of the legal scholars. In the effort to ascertain
the will of Allah, which is the essence of Muslim jurisprudence,
the *Ijtihad* of individual scholars was a human and therefore fallible

process. Its result could constitute only probable interpretations of Allah's will. But jurisprudence asserted that, when a rule was the subject of general agreement by the scholars, its acceptance was proof that it was correct, and that it thus represented as incontrovertible expression of the divine will. This principle obviously precluded further discussion on any point so settled.

Furthermore, where differences of doctrine between the various schools persisted, the notion of *Ijmas* carried to the point where it was held to cover these differences as equally possible and equally legitimate interpretations of the law but at the same time to deny the right to adduce any further solution. And it was because the jurists had thus agreed to differ that the four schools of law were regarded as equally orthodox definitions of the will of Allah. In each school, therefore, the current body of law embodied in the authoritative legal manuals written in the early medieval period came to be regarded as the final and perfect expression of the system of Allah's commandments. The role of future jurists was to be confined to the consolidation of this doctrine. There was no longer any need or scope for Ijtihad, and ultimately this attitude was expressed as an infallible consensus of opinion that "the door of Ijtihad was closed." From then on, all jurists were known as followers or imitators bound by the doctrine called *Taqlid* to follow the law expounded by the doctrine called *taqlid*. Of course, Shi'a doctrine provides some exceptions to this. But it must be kept in mind that Shi'a'ism also subordinates free inquiry to the limitations set by the authoritative pronouncements of an infallible Hidden (and coming) Imam.

As part of this body of crystallized law, the Koran had stressed the desirability of the husband's being able to provide for his several wives and of his treating them impartially. But, naturally perhaps under the prevailing cultural conditions, the import of these precepts had been minimized by interpretation, and they were generally regarded as imposing merely moral obligations upon the polygynous husband. For their breach, the law did recognize certain limited sanctions. The wife might be relieved of her duty of cohabitation, or the husband might be subject to minor forms of punishment. But the obligations were not construed as restricting in any way the exercise by the husband of his undisputed right to have more than one wife. In this as in all other respects, the law was artificially set in a rigid mold, not I may suggest, as the result of any incontrovertible axiom of the Islamic faith, but as the outcome of a complex historical process springing from the desire to set upon each and every detail of the law the stamp of divine approval.

So it is in this framework, that the classical Islamic concept of aw finally emerged as that of a law totalitarian in its terms and immutable, its authenticity guaranteed by the infallible Ijma. It was a concept of law that was to dominate Muslim thought until the past few decades of this century.

In modern times, the problem presented by the clash between the dictates of the legal system based upon a society of early medieval times and allegedly unchangeable and the demand of contemporary Muslim society naturally became acute. Only recently and in response to the West, the criminal law of the Sharia has been almost entirely abandoned in many Muslim countries in favor of codes of law based on Western models. In the realm of the family law, which was always regarded as a particularly vital and integral part of the religious faith, however, such an extreme solution has been not quite acceptable. Turkey, it is true, abandoned Sharia family law outright in 1927 and adopted in its place the Swiss Civil Code. The incorporation of Western models of education in Turkey and its implications, such as secularization and legal modernism, for Islam will be discussed in a later chapter. Nevertheless, it is significant to note that, over the past forty years, when such intense thought has been given to this problem, no single Muslim country has as yet seen fit to follow this example. Instead, conscientious endeavors have been made to adapt the Sharia to the needs of modern society. This process of legal modernism I shall now attempt briefly to outline on its principal features as they have developed in some Muslim societies.

Because of the strength of the classical concept of law, the reformers strove at first to remain within the bounds of the traditional doctrine of *Taqlid*, or imitation, and to base their reforms upon juristic principles recognized as legitimate by classical jurisprudence. The basis of their work was to define the position of the political authority vis-a-vis the Sharia law. This doctrine asserts that, although the political authority has no legislative power to modify or supercede the Sharia, it nevertheless has the power, and indeed the duty, to make supplementary administrative regulations to effect the smooth administration of law in general.

Two main types of such administration attracted the attention of the reformers. First, there was the power of the sovereign to define the jurisdiction of his courts. In general, the reformers argued, this power allowed him to codify the Sharia and, in particular, when there was a conflict of opinion among the jurists on a given point, to adopt and embody in the code that particular opinion among the existing variants that he deemed most suitable for application. Conflict of opinion within the Sharia is, as we have seen, reflected by the existence of four distinct schools of law whose varying doctrines are regarded as equally legitimate expressions of Allah's Law. It was therefore open to a Hanafi ruler in South-West Asia to select, and to order his courts to apply the doctrine of one of the other schools on a given point. It was on this juristic basis that the Ottoman Law of Family Rights took a first step toward the limitation of polygyny in 1927 by "selecting" the Hanbali doctrine governing stipulations in marriage contracts as better suited than the Hanafi doctrine to the needs and conditions of the time (Allen 1933). The Hanabalis, as I have already noted, are the only school that allow a wife to claim dissolution of her marriage if her husband marries a second wife in breach of a prior agreement not to do so.

The widespread use of this principle since 1927 has resulted in many changes in the law as traditionally applied in many Muslim societies. Peoples who are officially Hanafis are now governed by codes of law that represent eclectic amalgams of the doctrines of all the four schools.

The second limb of the doctrine of administrative regulations successfully utilized by the reformers was the recognized right of the sovereign to confine the jurisdiction of his courts, in the sense that might set limits to the competence of the Sharia tribunals by forbidding them to entertain certain types of cases on procedural grounds.

For an example of the subtle application of this principle in legal reform, let us turn to a sphere of the family law other than that of polygyny—to legitimacy. The one aspect of legitimacy in Sharia law that concerns us here is its importance in regard to succession. For the legitimate child is by law indefeasibly entitled to the bulk of the deceased father's estate while the illegitimate child is barred from any right at all (Goode 1963). When a child is born to a widow, whether or not he is legally regarded as the legitimate child of the deceased husband depends upon whether or not the law presumes that the child was conceieved during the husband's lifetime. The law therefore sets down a maximum period of gestation, which it presumes may possibly elapse between the conception of a child and its birth. If a child is born to a widow within this period it will be presumed to be the legitimate child of the deceased husband. This maximum period of gestation laid down in the authoritative manuals was two years according to the Hanafis, four years and more according to the other schools. From the point of view of modern medical knowledge of gestation, the harsh and inequitable results of this rule were obvious. In particular, the bulk of a deceased Muslim's estate might pass to a child who could not be his own child.

An Egyptian law of 1929 therefore declared that no disputed claim of legitimacy would be entertained by the courts, if it could be shown that the child concerned was born more than one year after the termination of the marriage between the mother of the child and the alleged father (Goode 1963). The jurisdiction of the courts in matters of legitimacy was confined to hearing cases in which the factual situation involved as involved as in accord with modern medical opinion. The rule of traditional Sharia law was not contradicted or denied as such, but by a procedural device the courts were precluded from applying the rule.

By such methods, far-reaching modifications were effected in the Sharia law as traditionally applied. And formally at any rate, the reforms had been accomplished within the framework of the doctrine of Taqlid, for it was the law as expounded in the medieval texts that was still accorded exclusive and binding authority. The limitations of such methods, however, are readily apparent, and eventually the desired reforms could not be supported by any shadow of traditional authority. At that stage, the reformers had perforce to abandon any pretense of Taqlid. They came to challenge the binding nature of the medieval manuals of law and the interpretations of the original sources recorded in them; they claimed the right to step beyond this corpus of juristic speculation and to interpret the Koran afresh in the light of modern needs and circumstances. They renounced the duty of Taqlid and claimed the right of Ijtihad.

The approach was of course met with the argument from traditional elements that it contradicted the infallible Ijma and as such was tantamount to heresy but its supporters argued that such Ijma did not exist at all—it being manifestly impractical to ascertain the views of each and every legal scholar throughout the far-flung territories of Islam in the ninth century, or alternatively, that if it did exist, it was not binding, for this amounted to the arrogation by a self-constituted human authority of a legal sovereignty that belongs only to Allah. Although scholars like Mohammed Abduh in Egypt at the turn of this century and Iqbal in Pakistan had already advocated a dynamic reinterpretation of the Koran as the basis for comprehensive legal reform, the reformers were very conscious that their activities constituted an outright break with the practical legal tradition of ten centuries standing, and so their first steps in this fruitful direction were hesitant and tentative (Iqbal 1934; Gibb 1955).

Their approach to the problem of polygyny centered upon the Koranic suggestions that a husband should be financially able to support his several wives and that he should treat them impartially. In 1953, the Syrian law of Personal Status interpreted the requirement of financial ability as a definite condition limiting the exercise of the right of polygyny (Anshen 1953). With this interpretation was coupled an administrative regulation requiring all marriages to be registered and further requiring permission of the court as a preliminary to such registration. The result was that a court would not give its permission for a second marriage unless it was satisfied that the husband was financially able to support more than one wife.

It may of course be argued that the only practical result of this reform was to make polygyny the privilege of the rich. Yet the real importance of the Syrian reform lies in its juristic basis and in the fact that a novel interpretation had been given to the text of the Koran. Once unlocked, the door of *ijtihad* was swung fully open by the Tunisian Law of Personal Status of 1957 (Goode 1963). This law interpreted the Koranic injunction regarding impartial treatment of co-wives in the same way that the Syrians had interpreted the requirement of financial ability—as a legal condition precedent to the very exercise of the right of polygyny and one that would naturally apply regardless of financial standing. But it is no longer within the discretion of the court to permit a polygynous marriage on the grounds that it is satisfied that the financial condition will be fulfilled. For the law goes on to state that in the circumstances of modern society it is impossible to treat several wives impartially to their mutual satisfaction; in technical language, there is a conclusive or irrefutable presumption of law that this essential precedent condition is incapable of fulfilment. Polygyny was therefore prohibited outright.

Such is the current condition of an allegedly immutable law in the Muslim world. Two considerations must be borne in mind. In the first place, these reforms are not put forward as deviations, occasioned by practical necessity from the ideal Islamic law, but as the contemporary expressions of that ideal law. And, in the second place, there is no uniformity in the method of legal modernism, or in its results throughout the Muslim world, and it is apparent that the process will tend initially at any rate, toward a growing diversity in Islamic legal practice conditioned by the varying reactions in the different areas to the stimuli of the modern life. This point is made quite clear, even on the one question of polygyny, by the three most recent reform enactments of Islamic law. The Moroccan law of 1958 merely gives the court the power to intervene retrospectively, by way of dissolution of the marriage, when a polygynous husband has failed to treat his wives impartially. The Iraqi law of 1960 goes further than the Syrian law in decreeing that the permission of the court is necessary for a second marriage and that such permission can be granted only when the husband meets the necessary financial criteria and when no inequality of treatment is to be feared (Harris 1958). Finally, the Muslim Family Laws Ordinance, promulgated in Pakistan in 1961, requires the permission of a duly constituted arbitration council for a second marriage

(Abbott 1968), under pain of penal and other sanctions, and states that such permission can be given only when the council is satisfied that the prospective marriage will be considered "necessary and just," it is obvious that the consent of the existing wife is extremely relevant, but such factors as the sterility, physical infirmity, or insanity of an existing wife are also specifically cited as relevant.

We are now perhaps in a position broadly to appreciate the significance of the Tunisian reform in the context of the phenomenon of legal modernism. In its simplest forms, the problem facing Muslim jurisprudence today is the same problem it has always faced, one that is inherent in its very nature—the need to define the relationship between the standards imposed by the religious faith and the mundane forces that activate society. At the one extreme is the solution adopted by classical jurisprudence, a divine, nomocracy under which religious principles were elaborated into a comprehensive and rigid scheme of duties to form the exclusive determinant of the conduct of society. The other extreme solution is that of secularism, adopted by Turkey, which relegates religious principles to the realm of the individual conscience and allows the forces of society unfettered control over the shape of the law. Neither of these solutions, can be acceptable to contemporary Muslim opinion generally. For, while the former is wholly unrealistic, the latter must inevitably be regarded as un-Islamic. Obviously, the answer lies somewhere between these two extremes in a concept of law as a code of behavior founded upon certain basic and immutable religious principles but, within these limits, responsive to change and permissive of such new standards and values as may prove more acceptable to current Muslim opinion than does indigenous tradition. Law, to be a living social force, must reflect the soul of its society. And the soul of present Muslim society is reflected neither in any form of outright secularism nor in the doctrine of the medieval textbooks. In its efforts to solve the problem of the clash between the dictates of traditional law and the demands of modern society, legal modernism, as it appears in its most extreme stage, the Tunisian reform rests upon the premise that the will of Allah was never expressed in terms so rigid or comprehensive as the classical doctrine maintained but that it enunciated broad general

principles that admit of varying interpretations and varying applications according to the conditions of the time. Modernism, therefore, is a movement toward a historical exegesis of the divine revelation and, as such, can find its most solid foundation in the early
historical growth of Sharia law that I have described. For recent
scholarship and research have demonstrated that Sharia law originated as the implementation of the precepts of divine revelation
within the framework of current social conditions, and in so doing
they have provided a basis of historical fact to support the ideology
underlying legal modernism. Once the classical theory is viewed
in its true historical-developmental perspective, as only one stage
in the evolution of the Sharia, modernist activities no longer
appear as a total departure from the one legitimate position but
preserve the continuity of Islamic legal tradition by taking up
again the attitude of the earliest jurists of Islam and reviving a
corpus whose growth had been artificially arrested, that had laid
dormant for a period of more than ten centuries.

It cannot be said, however, that legal modernism had yet reached the stage in which it provides a completely satisfactory
answer to the problems of law and society in the present-day Islam.
Traditionalist elements condemn some reformist activities like the
unwarranted manipulation of the text of divine revelation to force
from them meanings in accord with the preconceived purposes of
the reformers. This manipulation, argue the traditionalists, is in
substance, if not in form nothing less than the secularization of the
law. Modernist jurisprudence does in fact often wear an air of
opportunism, adopting *ad hoc* solutions out of expediency, and
does not yet rest upon systematic foundations or principles consis-
tently applied. "Socio-Cultural Engineers," which the modernists
certainly are, inasmuch as their activities are shaping the law to
conform to the needs of society. Yet if Islamic jurisprudence is to
remain faithful to its fundamental ideals, it cannot regard the
needs and aspirations of society as the exclusive determinants of
the law. These elements can legitimately operate to mold the law
only within the bounds of such norms and principles as have been
irrevocably established by divine command.

Looking to the future, therefore, it appears that the primary task
of Muslim jurisprudence is to ascertain the precise limits and impli-

cations of the original core of divine revelation. And this task will perhaps come to involve a restructuring of the traditional attitudes toward the reported precedents of the Prophet, not only in terms of their authenticity but also in terms of the nature of their authority, once authenticity is duly established. And it seems axiomatic that, when the precepts of divine revelation have been established, they must form the fundamental and invariable basis of any system of law that proposes to be a manifestation of the will of Allah.

It cannot be denied that certain specific provisions of the Koran, like the one that commands the amputation of the hand for theft, pose problems in the context of contemporary life for which the solution is readily apparent. But generally speaking, the Koranic precepts are ethical norms broad enough to support modern legal structures and capable of varying interpretations to meet the particular needs of time and place. And on this basis, it seems that Islamic jurisprudence can implement, in practical, realistic, and modernist terms, its basic and unique ideal of a way of life based on the command of Allah. Freed from the notion of the religious law expressed in totalitarian and uncompromising terms, jurisprudence could approach the problem of law and society in a different light. Instead of asking itself, as it had done since the tenth century and still does today, what concessions must be wrested from the law to meet the needs of society, it can adopt new terms of reference precisely opposite in intent, to determine what limitations religious principles set upon the frank recognition of social needs.

But however considerable the problems that still face Islamic jurisprudence may be, legal modernism has at least infused new life and movement into Sharia law and freed its congealed arteries from a state fast approaching total blockage. The era of Taqlid, of blind adherence to the doctrines of medieval scholars now appears as a protracted moratorium in Islamic legal history. It is hoped that stagnation would give increasing way to new vitality and potential for growth and positive, responsible transformation.

As mentioned before, Turkey had been the only Muslim country to substitute Islamic law totally with the civil code of Switzerland. Now, in view of the great strides that have been made in the law of other Islamic states, a few thinkers in Turkey have raised the question: Are not the other Muslim countries slowly doing what Turkey has done by revolution? To this the other Muslim countries such as Pakistan (Abbott 1968) reply that it was easy for Turkey to discard a system of law which it never regarded as part of her national-cultural heritage. To them, they say, the Sharia is an integral part of their cultural heritage which would not so easily be disclaimed. To Muslim nationalists, it is a matter of national pride that the Sharia should be preserved in order to maintain the continuity of the national heritage. Thus the modernization of the Sharia is not looked upon merely as another way of transforming the Muslim legal systems into Western secular systems. The Muslims are consciously trying to preserve those elements of the Sharia capable of survival by adapting them under the impact of Western law to modern conditions of life. No serious efforts are made to copy the Kemalist experiment in abolishing the Sharia totally.

Nor is the complete break with the past in the life of a nation, whether in the field of law or in any other system of social control, always a happy one. New regimes set up by revolutions must be maintained by force in order to prevent the continuity of past influences, but once such force or external control is relaxed through time, as recent experiences in Turkey have shown (see Chapters Seven and Eight), the people are likely to have recourse to past concepts and customs which are not so easy to obliterate in the life of a national culture. A system of law survives because it has adapted to the social, political, economic, and psychological conditions of life. The conditions may be modified by a government guided by some new ideology or philosophical ideas, but such a government can safely follow them only if it makes concessions to traditions and local conditions. Cultural change by its very nature is slow and requires a nexus with the past in order to insure healthy progress. A sudden break with the past may not always be the sure way for a nation to leap into a modern phase of progress.

SECULAR EDUCATION AND CULTURAL TRANSFORMATION: THE CASE OF TURKEY

CHAPTER EIGHT

SECULAR EDUCATION AND CULTURAL TRANSFORMATION: THE CASE OF TURKEY

As a phrase, "modernization in a Muslim society" begs more conceptual issues in fewer words than almost any other that has been discussed so far. Only the preposition seems straightforward. First, there are the much-discussed difficulties implicit in the notion of "modernization." Such difficulties have already been discussed in Chapter Three. Nevertheless, it is worth pointing out that the relationship between "modernization" and "Westernization," the usefulness of sorting cultural patterns and social practices into pigeonholes labeled "traditional" and "modern," the "progressive roles," certain "reactionary" institutions like the extended family, ascribed status, or personal clientship seem to play in some modernizing situations—all these elements have become recurrent concerns in the anthropological literature on the new states. Geertz's (1960:199-214) discussion of cultural change in Modjokuto, Lerner's (1964) observations and conclusions regarding the Near East including Turkey, Jacobs (1967) regarding Iran, are ample instances of such renewed interests. Second, with respect to a "society," considered as a total bounded unit, the question has been raised whether or not it can be a proper subject of scientific study at all. Or must we not instead resign ourselves to investigating particular ranges of social institutions—family, class, religion, and the specific relations obtaining among them, without attempting to talk about society as a "whole"? Some have gone so far as to suggest that such entities as "Turkish society" or "French society" do not even exist in any recognizable sense, that these terms are merely misleading names for political units and/or for states (Geertz 1968).

But of all the concepts alluded to so far, the concept "Muslim" seems to conceal the most radical difficulties, for there the sheer possibility of scientific analysis threatens to disappear. Some authorities on Islam, at least, are coming as a result of increasing awareness of the disparate character of "Islam" as it is practiced from place to place, and of the varying nature of the modern world's impact on different "Muslim" countries, to doubt whether in the religious realm there is either in empirical fact or in theory anything to which the name Islam can meaningfully be given (Smith 1966). Like some ancient parchment kept as an heirloom, my very problem thus threatens to crumble in my hands, as soon as ceasing simply to affirm its importance, I attempt actually to grasp it.

In countering this kind of stultifying historicism, which every significant increase in scholarly realism about social matters seems to bring with it, the anthropologist's response is always to turn again to the smaller canvas, for what seems vague and orderless may then take on more precise and regular outlines. One can overcome many of the apparent failings of "modernization," "society," and "Islam" as abstractions by applying them within the context of concrete examples. The value of such an example does not lie in its typicalness or representativeness, in the possibility of assimilating other cases directly to it. Rather, it lies in the fact that, by viewing social and cultural processes in limited and specific terms, one can isolate some features that are truly general, features that, when suitably adjusted to special circumstances, are relevant to the analysis of a wide range of cases. Whether or not they are in heaven, Islam, modernization, and society exist on earth. The problem is to know where to look for them.

I shall look for them at this point in Turkey and most particularly in the sphere of education there. This may seem an exceedingly odd choice. One that threatens to reduce serious intellectual problems to matters of mere pedagogy, and scholastic pedagogy at that. But in fact, the educational systems in all societies, especially the Muslim systems have been and are the master institutions in the perpetuation of a tradition and the creation of an Islamic society as well as the locus of the most serious present efforts to modernize that tradition and that society. Elsewhere in this book I have discussed Islamic law, and what role it has and can play in the modernization of Islamic societies.

In the Ottoman period, the Islamic religion was a unifying element in society and the very basis upon which the Ottoman State rested. Accordingly, religious schools and religious instruction in schools were unquestioned premises in the traditional Turkish theocratic ideology. Even Ziya Gokalp, the intellectual apostle of the new Turkish order, envisaged Islamic education as a basic ingredient of the education of the Turkish youth (Berkes 1964). On the other hand, Ataturk and his fellow-revolutionaries conceived of such an education as a stumbling block in the modernization of the new nation and as an integral part of the old order that must be stamped out. By a series of bold strokes, the theocratic edifice of the state had collapsed and with it all the supporting paraphernalia. In 1923, the Ministry of Education took over the administration and control of the religious schools and all their means of support (endowments and funds). In the same year, the teaching of religion was proscribed in all state schools, by the elimination of the august office of Sheykh-ul-Islam (the head of the Muslim community), and by the replacement of the Ministry of Religious Law with a Presidency of Religious Affairs under the prime minister (Berkes 1964). In 1928, Article 2 of the first Constitution of the Republic of Turkey, which had made Islam the state religion, was amended, providing for disestablishment; and in 1937, the principle of secularism was incorporated in the constitution. In the meantime, the jurisdiction of the courts of the Sharia had been taken over by the laiety, Western modeled courts, and a Turkish civil court, a virtual replica of the Swiss Civil Code had replaced the orthodox private Islamic laws. By 1930, what few secondary schools for religious leaders had survived went out of existence, and by 1933, the faculty of theology of Istanbul University was also abolished.

As time passed, the government took other steps to undermine religion in the society and its influence in education. In 1925, the wearing of the famous fez, a headgear which had become an important symbol of Islam in Turkey, was prohibited and all men were compelled by law to wear European-type hats; at the same time, a ban was proclaimed against the wearing of religious garments or insignia by any person who did not hold a religious office and against the famed *dervish* orders. In 1934, the wearing of religious vestments of any kind by any member, including clergymen, of any faith was proscribed except when such persons were in holy places or were conducting religious ceremonies.

One of the most revolutionary and far-reaching steps towards the religious orientation and re-education of the people was the language reform, namely, the change in the alphabet from Arabic to the Latin script. The romanization of the alphabet had pedagogical, cultural, nationalistic, and religious implications. Arabic was the language of the Koran, and the Arabic script symbolized the people's holy attachment to Islam. It was also the symbol which united the Muslim world and distinguished it from the world of "infidels." To the reformists it was a potent medium which chained the minds of Turks to the old order, to superstition, alien beliefs, and reaction. Moreover, it was a cumbersome vehicle for purposes of instruction, especially for the re-education of the entire nation. The change in the alphabet was followed by a systematic attempt to expurgate the language of all Arabic and Persian accretion and to develop a purely Turkish medium (at least non-Islamic) of communication. An intensive campaign to instruct the nation in the reading and writing of the new script followed, and Ataturk himself bceame the "chief instructor of the School of the Nation." In 1929, Arabic and Persian were prohibited as subjects of instruction in the curriculum of the secondary schools; and history books were re-written with major emphasis placed upon the ethnic background of the Turks and with exaggerated and dubious theories about their origin and influence in the world. The Turkicization of the language and the laicization of religion were part of the general process of modernizing the society and establishing a sense of national identity for the Turks. Every single aspect of reform was justified on nationalistic grounds and as a concerted effort to indicate that the Turks were, or had the potential to be, as modernized as any other nation of the world. There is no question that the changes effected almost overnight were dramatic. In outward form, the face of the nation along with the structure of society was almost totally transformed; a tradition and a structure reaching far back in the middle ages all but disappeared. But to what extent Ataturk had succeeded completely in secularizing the new nation, or indeed education and the minds of of the people, is today not so clear as it may have seeemed during the heyday of Islamic reform.

The issue of religion or the role of Islam in the new state was quite dormant until the forties. With Turkey's transition from a one-party to a multiparty system (from 1946-1950), religion again emerged as a political and cultural issue. The process of liberalizing restrictions on religion imposed during the Ataturk regime through positivistic secularist policies, has continued up to the present. In the past twenty years or so, Turkey has been groping with the problem of readjusting its nationalistic ideology and policies to the pressing demands for a more positive approach to Islam as an educational and social institution. Not unexpectedly, of course, the liberalization of religion became a political slogan for vote-getting, as religion was still an important part of the lives of the people, especially the non-urban population. Indeed, part of the strength of the Democratic Party, which was voted into power in 1950 and remained so until the revolution of 1960, lay in its promises and policies concerning religion in schools and in the lives of the people (Berkes 1964). However, the revival of interest in religion was part of ideological reaction against the strict secularism of the republic by a diverse group of individuals who felt that the moral basis of the society was being corroded and that the youth were being brought up in a moral vacuum. In a culture which had deep roots in an Islamic past, it was natural that there would be open criticism of the restrictions imposed by the government once the lid was lifted and a more pluralistic approach was being followed.

The form which the revived issues took varied. There were those who had a fond yearning for the religious and simple life of the past, and who felt that the modern secular society had lost some of the spiritual strength so necessary for its survival. The intellectuals in this group claimed that Islam was not reactionary, that it was supportive of "science" and modern institutions. In language reminiscent of the position taken by advocates of the value of religious instruction in secular societies of the West, the "conservatives" in Turkey have argued that Islam would elevate the moral standards of the youth and of society. For, after all, is not the ultimate aim of any educational system the creation of moral and responsible beings? Moreover, this group has argued that Islam would more effectively combat any "leftist" tendencies in the society, and would restore the fundamentals which were characteristic of a powerful past Turkish society.

Another more "moderate" position has been espoused by people who wanted to liberalize religion by making it a matter of individual conscience and rights without any planned proscriptions by the government. At the other extreme were the staunch secularists who stuck to the republican ideology, not because they opposed Islam, but rather because Islam went beyond matters of faith by regulating many other activities of the individual in the social and cultural domains. Islam was too dogmatic and reactionary as an institution and, hence, was inimical to the modernization and development of the country (Karpat 1959:271-278).

One of the first openly discussed questions was that of religious education. After a full-dress debate in the Grand National Assembly in 1949, courses in Islam were permitted in the fourth and fifth classes of the elementary schools (Berkes 1964). At first the courses on religion were to be optional and only for those children whose parents had indeed asked for such courses; they soon became compulsory for all Muslim children in the fourth and fifth grades, except in the lower classes, such instruction remained optional. By 1950, the great majority of primary school children took the courses in religious education (Robinson 1963). Two other developments in religious education during this period were significant.

In 1949, a Faculty of Divinity was opened at the University of Ankara, under the control of the Ministry of Education. Government scholarships were provided for a large number of students. At about the same time, secondary schools for the training of religious leaders *(imam hatib okullari)* were re-established, with a six-year course following the elmentary schools. By 1961-62, there were nineteen middle level religious schools enrolling about five thousand students, seventeen lycee (high school) level schools with about one thousand students, and one higher Islamic institute with two hundred students (Robinson 1963).

There have been several other indications of a religious revival since the post-war period. More mosques were built, and attendance in them increased considerably. After the Democratic Party came to power, it allowed the *azan* (the Muslim call to prayer) to be read in Arabic instead of Turkish, and excerpts from the Koran to be read on the radio, and a greater number of Muslims made the annual pilgrimage to Mecca. There was even some relaxation in the wearing of the religious garb: religious functionaries were allowed to wear the beret, a social equivalent of the turban (Lewis 1961:410-418). In the field of education, acrimonious debate in the press and in the Turkish congress raged around the inclusion of courses in religion in the middle schools, the lycee, and other schools. In 1956, a one-hour weekly course in Islam was introduced into the first and second classes of the middle schools, and religious instruction was allowed in the "normal schools." Since 1950, there has been a dramatic increase in special courses of approximately a year's duration in the reading of the Koran (Maynard 1961:71).

Explanations and assessment of the renewed interest in religion and of its possible future significance, have been made with a great deal of caution. From the political standpoint some see the movement for the liberalization of religion as a natural consequence of the development of "democracy" and the multiparty system. This, together with what seemed to be a genuine interest to reform Islam itself by "purifying" and "modernizing" it, would be a salutary sign and would not jeopardize the progress toward modernization. Yet as Karpat points out, the liberalization of Islam may have been premature, in view of the fact that secularism had not as yet penetrated deeply into the lives and thoughts of all the segments of the Turkish population (1959:288).

Others seek to discount the significance of this religious interest for the social and cultural development of the country. Staunch secularists feel that the religious movement was fanned by survivors of the Ottoman past who had a sentimental attachment to tradition. They argue when this generation disappears, so will any reactionary religious tendencies. Bernard Lewis (1961:417-418) and Frederick Frey (1964:223) reject this viewpoint, arguing that, despite some of the policies of the revolutionary government of Ataturk and the adoption of laicism as one of the elements of the ideology of the republic, Islam had continued to be deeply imbedded in the minds and lives of the people, especially among the peasant masses. According to Lewis, "the deepest Islamic roots of Turkish life and culture are still alive, and the ultimate identity of Turk and Muslim in Turkey is still unchallenged." Under such circumstances, Lewis hopes that the Turks will find a workable compromise between Islam and modernism; otherwise, if the reactionaries gain ascendancy, there will be a regression and Turkey "will slip back into the darkness from which she so painfully emerged" (1961:418).

There is some other evidence on the question of religion in Turkey which might cast more light on any speculation about the furture or on statements concerning the process of modernization. The few studies on Turkish villages that are available indicate that among villagers, Islam continues to be a powerful force in regulating the activities of life and in the system of belief about reality, the family, the individual, education, and the state. In his detailed study of the social structure of a central Anatolian village, Paul Stirling observed that villagers refer directly to religious authority to support almost every social rule, that the state or the government is still thought of the as ultimate religious authority, and generally, that almost every aspect of the social organization is related directly or indirectly to Islam (Stirling 1965). Stirling concludes: "It was my impression that for the villagers the most important characteristic of their society, and the one most resistant to innovation was their allegiance to Islam, and since their beliefs cover so wide a field, they constitute a powerful support for the whole social order" (Stirling 1965). Pierce echoed the same idea: "The villagers do not make a distinction, common to Americans and Europeans in general, between the religious and the secular. Islam is a way of life and is the dominant factor in the making of any decision, no matter how slight, in the mind of the villagers" (1964:87).

On the other hand, some observers have found that, although there is still a strong attachment to Islam, there is also an acceptance of innovation, social change, machines, secular schools, and so on, and that the possibility of a religious conservative reaction to the secular state is doubtful. Rather, Robinson observes, the Anatolian "was beginning to reposition his religion so as to be relevant to the modern world" (Robinson 1963:201-206). Another writer reports that in Hasanoglan, the authority and prestige of the *imam* has diminished considerably in the past thirty years (Yasa 1957:166).

In assessing the cultural and social significance of Islam among villagers, it must be remembered that this large segment of the Turkish population is still a "non-mobilized" mass. Strong bifurcations still exist between the rural peasant groups and the urban dwellers, and between the educated urban elite and an illiterate village population. Although the peasant group possesses the right to vote, and indeed a large percentage has voted in recent elections, the distance between the "rulers" and the "ruled" is still great, the latter for the most part accepting the policies and directions of the former, as in previous periods. Consequently, the future of Islam depends to a large extent on the attitudes of the urban population, the intelligentsia, and the elite. The situation of these segments of the population also seems to be uncertain. Throughout the period of the republic, urban classes have been exposed to greater amounts of education and the positive-secularistic campaign of the revolutionary government. Since education has been used to sustain the revolutionary ideology, a stronger attachment to secularism among the urban (more particularly the urban educated classes), a weaker hold of orthodox Islam on their lives, or a synthesis between Islam and modernism might be expected.

Unfortunately, information on the religious attitudes of these groups is rather limited. But on the basis of what is available, it could be said that at least among the more highly educated urban groups, especially in cosmopolitan centers like Ankara, Istanbul, and Izmir, the secular ideology of Ataturkism has taken strong roots. In the survey on the cultural value systems in the lycee-level institutions (aged 15 to 18), Frey found a strong secularism. According to him, this important school population refers most readily "to the tenets of the revolution and its conceptions of modernity, very seldom to religious values and principles" (1964). For example, only two per cent of the sampled students would, as parents, try to teach religious values to their children; only seven per cent mentioned religion as an activity which would satisfy them most; and a religious career was ranked very low in terms of prestige. The only time that the students showed pro-religious interests was when about sixty-nine per cent of the group indicated that they felt "some form of religious belief (was) necessary to a fully mature approach to life" (Frey 1964:226). Taking an even more select group (students at Robert College, Istanbul, and at the Faculty of Political Science of the University of Ankara), Hyman, Payaslioglu and Frey found an even weaker attachment to religious, in contrast to nationalistic, values (Hyman et al.: 1958). Only one per cent of these university students mentioned accomplishments in the area of religion as something that would bring the greatest pride; an even lower percentage stated that they would consider "loss of religious faith" as one of the two worst things that could conceivably happen to them; and religion ranked the lowest—lower than amusement and local citizenship activities" —on a rating of the importance of six sectors of life.

Hyman and his associates found that sixty-nine per cent of the sampled students indicated that they considered some form of religious orientation or belief necessary for the attainment of "a fully mature philosophy of life." Particularly revealing, however, was that even among such a highly select and highly educated group, fourteen per cent gave *kismat* (predestination) as the person's probable cause of death, this answer being one of the top three reasons given. The authors resolve this seeming paradox by saying that "some of the central precepts or philosophical content of traditional religion could well persist," even though certain religious practices "might well conflict with other values." Nevertheless,

comparing the responses on Turkish Universit y youths in these
two institutions with Gillespie and Allport's findings among youths
of other countries, they concluded that "the Turhish students are
only slightly more religious than Americans, and considerably less
religious than German and Italian youth. This is the last home
of the Caliph" (1955).

Orthodox Islam, in the Ottoman period, encompassed more
than matters of religious dogma, it also had political, social and
cultural connotations. It was both a religious and cultural philosophy, and it minutely regulated even the interpersonal relations
of the members of the society. The Kemalist revolution substituted
a secular state for the traditional Islamic theocracy, and curbed
the power of religion as an institution by fiat. Moreover, Ataturk
sought to inculcate a spirit of independence, a rational "scientific"
approach to life, and a positive feeling that the individual is
capable of shaping his own destiny and combat the vicissitudes of
his existence. The followers of Ataturkism are still too entrenched
in positions of political power for any religious reaction to take
place; and since 1923, a new generation of Turks has been educated in secular schools and "socialized" in nationalism and
"laicism." Nevertheless, although there may be no foreseeable
danger to upset the secular state, the persistence of traditional
Islamic attitudes and values slow the pace of modernity (Lerner
1964:43). In addition to kismat (predestination), and to certain
attitudes of the large village population, the study of lycee students
also reveals that certain traditional patterns of authority and
family relationships seem to persist even among such a selected and
highly educated group.

The traditional Ottoman Islamic society was based on an
authoritarian normative pattern. This was reflected in the relationships between the individual and the government (the sultan, the
officials, the village elders), between man and woman, husband and
wife, father and son, older and younger brother, and so on. In all
interpersonal relationships there was the same deferential attitude
by those of "inferior" to those "superior" status. These patterns
of relations were regulated in no small degree by Islam. Through
several reforms, Ataturk sought to substitute a democratic regime
for the Ottoman political absolutism and break down authorita-

rianism. It is well known, of course, that, although political institutions were changed, an absolutistic pattern of government (Ataturk, or the one-party system) continued until the emergence of the multiparty system in the forties (Berkes 1964). Even after that, and in view of another revolution and several abortive coup d'etats in the sixties, whether democracy has taken roots in the Turkish republic is not clear. More will be said about this later. On the question of authoritarianism, it has quite probably been weakened by the many cultural changes, the new views about education, the content of the curriculum, and the campaigns to introduce Western cultural values as well as Western symbols.

Research in this area, however, is limited, and the extent to which patterns of authority have changed has not been adequately determined. The few inconclusive studies that are available suggest that changes may indeed have taken place since the establishment of the republic and secularism. Contrasting what he calls the n-Achievement levels as gauged from children's stories in Turkey and Iran, McClelland found that Turkey ranked higher than Iran. Considering that the two countries have essentially similar background characteristics (especially the fact that they are both overwhelmingly Islamic) and that Turkey has attained a much higher degree of economic development, McClelland adduces "concern for higher achievement" as a possible explanation for the differential rates of growth between the two countries. He reasons: since low n-Achievement among sons has been found to be correlated with authoritarian fathers and since, according to Islamic tradition, Islamic societies are strongly dominated by the father, then the explanation for the differential levels of n-Achievement between Turkey and Iran must be sought in the extent to which the authority of the father has been maintained or has been undermined. McClelland then asserts that certain institutional and ideological changes carried out in Turkey since the revolution have indeed undermined the strong domination of the father. Thus he explains the differences between the two countries. Some of the institutional changes, which helped break down the strong male domination, were the abolition of the fez, "traditional symbol of male dignity," the separation of Islam and State—consequently, the replacement of Islamic law by civil law which altered the legal status of marriage—and the granting of rights to women. Furthermore, the organization of the new army and the establishment of village institutes (Vexliard and Aytach 1964:41-47) emancipated the boys from their autocratic fathers. Under ideological changes McClelland includes: (*a*) patriotism, which meant a shift in loyalty from father to nation or the "generalized other"; (*b*) modification of the traditional theme of trickery "in the direction of positive achievement," which undermined the belief that people cannot be trusted and that everybody is out to get you"; (*c*) modifications of people's perceptions of government authority or of how society affects one's life, which resulted in perceiving authority in more positive than negative terms (McClelland 1963:152-181).

McClelland's approach to the analysis of national characteristics (what he calls "content analysis of organized verbal or artistic symbol systems") and applications to problems affecting modernization and cultural transformation in the Muslim world is quite novel and intriguing. But his analysis of the Turkish situation must be looked at with some degree of caution and largely as a hypothesis that needs further substantiation. McClelland's approach and study pose several questions. To what extent do children actually internalize the values which are found in the "moral" of children's stories, and to what extent do they actually bring about changes in children's perceptions of authority? What evidence is there that the institutional and ideological changes during the republican period did indeed undermine the domination of male and/or the father, or contribute to a higher concern for individual achievement? For example, McClelland's assumption that the abolition of the fez undermined traditional "male dignity" might be questioned. The fez was more of a religious symbol signifying the "Muslimness" of the Turks. The present-day European hat is as much a male symbol as the old fez. Also, the separation of children from their families for service into the army was as much a characteristic of the Ottoman Islamic past as it is of the Turkish present. Further, the actual effect of the village institutes is difficult to assess. For one thing their duration was short (less than fifteen years); for another, the number of students who attended them was relatively small, in that a total of 17,162 diplomas were awarded (Vexliard and Aytach 1964), and all in all such institutions existed only in twenty-one villages. Although the village institutes represented an important experiment in the attempts to elevate the cultural level of the villagers and to bridge the gap between an educated elite and an uneducated populace, and although they provided an avenue for social mobility among the village youth, statements about their role in breaking down the traditional patterns of authority must to some extent be speculative. Finally, the different kinds of "morals" that McClelland finds in the Turkish and Iranian stories and his assumptions that the Iranian tales are more representative of the Islamic tradition or that they correspond to the Ottoman Turkish tradition might be questioned. In other words, for his interpretations, assuming they are correct, to have any validity, the stories to which Turkish children were exposed during the pre-revolutionary period (i.e. during the period of male autocracy and authoritarianism in the society) must also be examined.

McClelland conceded that the ideological and institutional changes in Turkey may have been more effective in cities rather than in villages, although he maintains that the new norms were known nationwide. However, impressionistic accounts and some empirical studies of this aspect of Turkish folk culture reveal that basic value patterns among the masses of the population have not altered to any substantial degree, and that the effects of secularism are primarily visible in the urban settings. Makal paints a dismal and discouraging picture of the Turkish village culture (1954). He suggests that the people of Nurguz, in central Turkey, are mere modern shadows of the bucolic and "primitive" Ottoman Anatolian peasant. Almost all the traditional modes of thinking, behaving, and feeling seem to have been totally unaffected by the ideology of modernity. The same fatalism, the same patterns of authority, the same suspicion about the outsider and the government official, and the same customs and superstitions of pre-republican days still exist (Makal 1954:11, 64, 68). Pierce (1964:78) observes that "status is acquired primarily by growing old." And Stirling notes that existing patterns of authority between the sexes are justified on religious grounds (1965).

Admittedly, such places do not represent the whole of rural

Turkey, nor all the villages of central Anatolia. Robinson, for example, reports that when he visited Alishar in 1949, he noticed many "physical changes" since 1932 (1963), and Daniel Lerner's Balgat changed from a "traditional" peasant community to a suburb of Ankara in four years. Yet Balgat cannot be taken as typical or as reflecting a countrywide change for the simple reason that it is so close to a fast-growing metropolitan center which is also the capital of Turkey. Nor does Robinson's Alishar represent "physical," let alone "normative," changes in the country as a whole. Indeed, while pointing to the quick transformation of Balgat, Lerner also notes that the "traditionals" in Turkey far outnumber the "moderns" and the "transitionals." According to him, they compose "well over half" (about 60 per cent) of the Turkish population "even today." And his descriptions of their "psychic traits" as well as their outlook on life, is not substantially dissimilar from Makal's observations. Their institutions, Lerner writes, "usually authoritarian, patriarchal, changeless; the values they enjoin are loyalty, obedience, inertia. The whole complex forms a 'courage culture,' in which absence of curiosity is a primary component 'theirs not to reason why, theirs but to do or die' " (Lerner 1964:133).

Turning to an urban and highly educated group, the Hyman and Frey surveys (1958:224-225) depict the Turkish youth as quite authoritarian. Using the Gillespie and Allport (1955) item to gauge authoritarian values (viz. "the world is a hazardous place, in which men are basically evil and dangerous") the Hyman survey showed that thirty-nine per cent of the respondents in the Ankara University group expressed agreement. This figure is higher than what Gillespie and Allport found in the national groups, except in countries like Egypt. The writers conclude that "while that aspect of the value constellation involving political absolutism seems dissipated in the present Turkish groups, the authoritarian aspect seems to have persisted" (Hyman et al., 1958:285). Although on the same item the Frey survey also indicated a high degree of authoritarianism among lycee students, the author expresses doubt that such students were as authoritarian as the general population. Furthermore, according to him, although authoritarianism is characteristic of the Turkish political system, "it tends to be counteracted by a strong sense of solidarity and by a growing ideological commitment to democratic forms, also inculcated by the school system" (Frey et al., 1968:224-225).

Such findings, however valuable they may be in exploring certain values among Turkish youth, must be examined and interpreted with a great deal of caution. In seeking to measure or assess attitudes and values in Muslim societies through the application of instruments validated in Western, culturally and politically different societies, there obviously is the danger of drawing hasty conclusions or reading the same meanings into the responses made in Western settings. This caveat must be entered particularly in the case of the aforementioned Turkish youth on items pertaining to authoritarianism, insecurity, and so on. The relatively high incidence of authoritarian responses among Turkish youth, as indeed among youth in other Muslim societies, may reflect ideological-structural, rather than personality factors of characteristics. A verbal response by a Turkish youth to a questionnaire item which in another culture setting might be interpreted as a psychological trait produced by a certain pattern of relationships, or as manifested in actual behavior, might indeed represent a standard superficial reaction to a persistently advocated idea. However, based upon the available and the outer manifestations of the Turkish culture today, one can reasonably well argue that this Muslim society began to lift itself up (culturally) in all its socio-cultural dimensions, when it initiated the separation of Islam from the realm of polity and to introduce techno-scientific ideas in the framework of a non-Muslim education in its system. The implications for political development as they correlate with modernity will be examined in the next chapter. It is nonetheless hoped that this exploratory investigation into such areas as authority, distrust, security, and the like will spur further research on the cultural-psychological aspects of education in Turkey and in other Muslim societies.

The significance of education in building the new nation was repeatedly stressed by Ataturk and by all other modern Turkish thinkers and political leaders. A cardinal tenet of the revolutionary ideology and of the new Turkish leaders who would initiate and carry through changes in order to transform traditional patterns, beliefs and practices, and to establish a modern, democratic and secular state. The educational system, particularly certain types of schools, were assigned the major task of training such "new Turks." Far from undermining the significance of education for political ascendancy and social differentiation, the policies of the republic carried forward and indeed strengthened this feature of the Ottoman legacy (Frey 1965). The difference between the Ottoman and the republican periods, insofar as this aspect of the school-society relationship was concerned, lay not in the role assigned to education for social mobility, class differentiation, and more pertinently, leadership status; rather, they lay mostly in the kind of educational or professional specialization that facilitated access to positions of political leadership, and in the types of institutions and the occupational categories from which political leaders were recruited.

Since the emergence of the idea of Turkish national state, Turkish leaders have conceived of the schools as prime agencies in developing national consciousness, ideologies, values, and behaviors different from what had existed before and aimed at the overall transformation of the political organization of the country. As stated earlier, the idea of Turkish nation-state was not even introduced until the latter part of the nineteenth century. But the idea of the Turkish secular nation with clearly defined physical boundaries, with a common culture, a common language, a common religion was a twentieth century one and for all meaningful purposes a post-revolutionary phenomenon. To accomplish this task the schools were assigned a great deal of importance.

Ayal suggests that "new ideologies take hold either when a major crisis which undermines the validity of an existing value system is already occurring, or when a creeping breakdown of old values is taking place and the bearers of the new ideology use it as a weapon to accelerate the breakdown" (1966:231). The case of Turkey was indeed an illustration of this hypothesis. It is also argued that "nationalist ideology is particularly effective in supporting logically irreconcilable formulae—one of the most important and unique roles of ideology" (Ayal 1966:232). Foremost in the school's responsibility for the education of the Turkish youth has been the inculcation of nationalistic sentiments. Objec-

tives such as the training of youth "to feel the honor of being a
son of the Turkish race," to respect the national flag, "to protect
the esteem of the glorious Turkish history," to appreciate "the
great Turks whose service have made the great Turkish nation,"
to be bound by the principles of the Turkish Revolution, "to
preserve," as Ataturk put it, "and defend the National Independence of the Turkish Republic," and so on, continue to be important goals of national education. All political parties in Turkey
have proclaimed these as being central goals of education (Robinson 1950).

Instruction in schools, aimed at the development of patriotism
and other Turkish nationalistic ideological attitudes, takes the
form of both formal and informal activities, that is, courses in
civics, history, and Turkish, and the observation of national holi-
days, national celebrations, and so on. An example of the more
formalized nationalistic instruction is the content and emphasis of
the lycee courses in history. In each of the three lycee classes,
special emphasis is placed upon the history of the Turkish Republic (the Revolutionary War, the establishment of the republic, the
revolutionary ideology, the developments since 1923, etc.), and on
the origins, migrations and empire-building of the Turkish "race."
One of the explicit objectives of the history course is to "prepare
citizens with a national conciousness and feeling" (Maynard 1961:
331). In pursuing this objective, linking the development of the
Turkish "race" with that of the Turkish nation is stressed.
"Racism" is "a strong element in Turkish nationalism." In history textbooks, the word "motherland" sometimes refers to
Central Asia (with racial connotations, since the Turks originated
there) and sometimes to Anatolia, where the Turkish nation was
born (Maynard 1961).

Precisely how successful have the schools been in this aspect of
secular-political education of the Turkish youth? Based on several
impressionistic studies, the Turkish youth as well as the Turkish
people could be said to display strong nationalistic attitudes and
beliefs. Turkish nationalism is no longer the dream of a few
visionary utopian intellectuals; it is an activating force pervading
the entire fabric of society and influencing the course of Turkish
development. In the words of a Turkish political scientist: "natio-

nalism is the foundation of the Republic and a basic tenet in the program of all political parties....In internal affairs, nationalism became the supreme force dominating all activities in the society, visualizing problems and moulding ideas in the light of its own conception" (Karpat 1959:251). Turkish nationalism, like most of Turkey's modernization concepts and institutions, originated in the West. Some of the most influential Turkish nationalists like Ziya Gokalp were trained in the West (France). But like such concepts and institutions, it has been substantially transformed in accordance with Turkish cultural and historical conditions and the revolutionary ideologies. Indeed the concept is still undergoing change and adjustment. Nevertheless, it should be quite obvious by now that secularism initiated a new beginning through education in Turkey. The result has been a gradual shift from a prescriptive orientation to a principial, which this author considers one single overriding feature of the Western techno-scientific cultural tradition. The model proposed in the following chapter will be based on these two sets of assumptions.

THE BEGINNING OF TRANSFORMATION:
FROM PRESCRIPTIVE TO PRINCIPIAL

CHAPTER NINE

THE BEGINNING OF TRANSFORMATION: FROM PRESCRIPTIVE TO PRINCIPIAL

THE PROCESS OF development and modernization of Islamic societies such as Turkey, which will be considered here, involves
changes in the value systems as well as economic, political, educational, and social structural changes. In traditional Muslim
societies, the value system tends to be, as we have already seen,
what Becker calls "prescriptive" (Becker 1957:128). A prescriptive
system is characterized by a comprehensiveness and specificity of
the value commitments and by its consequent lack of flexibility,
discussed in Chapter Five. In Muslim systems, motivation is frozen,
so to speak, through commitment to a vast range of relatively
specific religious norms governing almost every dimension of life
(Kerr 1966). Islam, as I have already pointed out, is characterized by such a range of norms. Most of these specific norms,
usually those governing social institutions, are thoroughly integrated with a religious system (Islam), which invokes ultimate
sanction for every infraction and deviation from the norm. Thus,
changes in economic, political, and educational institutions in the

Muslim systems tend to have religious implications. Furthermore, because of the very close nature of state and religion, deviation in Islamic states is not only considered a political revolt but also a religious sin (Jacobs 1967). In other words, changes will and must involve Islamic religious sanctions.

Yet the Islamic society, when faced with grave dislocations consequent to Western contact, or internal pressures, must make major alterations in its institutional structure if it is to survive. What changes must be made in the organization of the structure and value system of Islam so that the developmental-modernizing changes must and can succeed?

I propose that the value system and the structure of Islam must change from a "prescriptive"-Islamic to a "principial"-secular type. The concepts "prescriptive" and "principial" have been adapted from Howard Becker (1957:128-129). Islamic societies, as we have already examined, tend to have a normative system, in which a comprehensive, codified (Koranic-Sharia), and uncodified (*hadith*) set of relatively specific norms governing concrete behavior. But in the Western society, an area of flexibility must be gained in economic, political, and social life in which specific norms may be determined in considerable part by short-term exigencies in the realm of behavior, or by functional requisites of the relevant social sub-systems. Ultimate or religious values may lay down the basic principles of social behavior; thus such a normative system is called "principial," but the religious system does not attempt to regulate economic, political, and social life in great detail, as in Islamic prescriptive societies.

Looking at this process another way, we may say that there must be a differentiation between religion and ideology, between ultimate values and proposed ways in which these values may be put into effect. In Islamic societies there is no such discrimination. Differences of opinion on legal, social, and economic policy is taken to imply differences as to religious commitment. The social innovator becomes a religious heretic. But in the Western society, there is a differentation between the levels of religious and cultural ideology which makes possible greater flexibility at both levels (Horowitz 1964:363).

How is the normative system in an Islamic society to be changed from prescriptive to principial, and how is the differentiation of the religious and ideological levels to be effected, especially in the face of the Islamic barriers and other components of the traditional culture in the Muslim society. I would like to assert that only a new religious-reformist initiative, only a movement which claims religious ultimacy for itself, can successfully challenge the inhibiting nature of the old value system and its Islamic base. The new movement, which arises from the necessity to make drastic cultural changes in the light of new conditions is essentially ideological and political in nature (see Chapter Three). But, arising as it does in a society in which the ideological level is not yet recognized as having independent legitimacy, the new movement must take on a religious coloration in order to meet the old Islamic system on its own terms. Even when such a movement is successful in effecting major structural changes in the Islamic society and freeing motivation formerly inhibited in traditional patterns so that considerable flexibility in economic and political life is attained, the problem posed by its own partly religious origin and its relation to the traditional Islamic religious system may still be serious indeed.

Let us turn to the example of Turkey. Ottoman Turkey in the 18th century was a non-secular traditional Islamic society with a prescriptive value system. Virtually, all spheres of life were theoretically under the authority of Islamic law (Berkes 1964:9). Indeed the government was supposed to have an area of freedom within the law. But this freedom had become narrowly restricted. Precedents of governmental procedure were tacitly assimilated to the Islamic law or the Sharia (Berkes 1964:15).

Beginning with Selim III in the late 18th century, a series of reforming sultans and statesmen attempted to make major changes in Turkish culture in an effort to cope with the increasingly desperate internal and external conditions. While some changes were made, especially in areas remote from the central stronghold of the Sharia, such as the administrative machinery, the reforming party was unable to attain any ultimate legitimation in the eyes of the people and although Turkish society was shaken to its foundation, periods of reform alternated with periods of blind reaction in which reformers were executed or banished (Lewis 1961).

The last of these reactionary periods was that of the rule of Sultan Abdul Hamid II, who was overthrown in 1908 by a coup of young army officers whom we know as the "Young Turks." By this time it had become clear to leading intellectuals that more was needed than another interim of needed reform. They saw that a basic change in the cultural foundation of Turkish society was demanded if the long delayed changes in economic and political structure were to be affected. Some felt that a modern purified Islam could provide the new cultural basis, but orthodox Islam was so deeply imbedded in the fabric of traditional society (as is the case in many Islamic societies today) that the Islamic modernists found little response in the religious dimension. Others looked to Western liberal democracy as a satisfactory foundation. Hence the introduction of the lycee system of education. Those sensitive to the mind of the Turkish masses, however, pointed out that the Turkish people would never accept a value system that was so obviously "made abroad" and which could so easily be condemned by the conservative forces of Islam with the stigma of unbelief (Berkes 1964).

It was Ziya Gokalp, a sociologist much influenced by Durkheim who actually championed Turkish nationalism as the only satisfactory cultural foundation for the new Turkey (Lewis 1964). Gokalp made the referent for all symbols of ultimate value in society itself. His answer to the religious conservatives such as the ulema was that the true Islam was that of the Turkish folk, not the established religious hierarchy which was largely educated in the Arabic and Persian languages, rather than the Turkish language. Here at last was an ideology to which the people could respond with emotion and which could challenge Islamic conservatism on its own ground.

But the course of world history did as much as Gokalp's eloquence to decide in favor of the nationalist alternative for Turkey. Not only did World War I strip Turkey of her empire but the subsequent invasions of Anatolia threatened the very life of the nation itself. Mustafa Kemal who led the ultimately successful effort to national resistance partly chose and partly was impelled to make the nation the central symbol in his subsequent drive for development and modernization. As a result, the highest value and central symbol for the most articulate sections of the Turkish people became not Islam but Turkism, or nationalism, or Kemalism, or simply "the Revolution." Having a strong national and personal charismatic legitimacy, Mustafa Kemal, later known as Ataturk—father of Turkey—was able to create a far-reaching cultural revolution in which the place of Islam in the Turkish society was fundamentally altered. We may note some of the landmarks in this revolution in which the place of Islam was so substantially transformed.

In 1924, the office of the Caliph was abolished (Berkes 1964:460). In the same year, all religious (Mosque) schools were closed or converted into the secular schools. The teaching of Islam was withdrawn from the curriculum of schools and made optional for those who desired to study religion (see Chapter Six). The most important change of all took place in 1926: the Sharia Law along with Muslim civil law was abandoned and the Swiss Civil Code adopted almost without change. Finally, in 1928, the phrase in the constitution stating that the religion of Turkey is Islam was deleted and Turkey was declared a secular state (Berkes 1964:461).

That the Turks were so deeply conscious of what they were doing is illustrated by the following quotation from Mohmud Essad, the Minister of Justice, under whom the Islamic law was abandoned:

> The purpose of law is not to maintain the old customs or beliefs which have their source in religion, but rather to assume the economic and social unity of the nation.

> When religion has sought to rule human societies, it has been the arbitrary instrument of sovereigns, despots, and strong men. In separating the temporal and the spiritual, modern civilization has saved the world from numerous calamities and has given to religion an imperishable throne in the consciences of behavior (Allen 1935:34).

This quotation illustrates well enough the transition from prescriptive to principial society and the differentiation of religion and ideology as two distinct levels. It is clear that the relatively great advances of Turkish society in economic, political, educational, and the other spheres of cultural life are based on this new cultural foundation. But implicit in Essad's words are some of the yet unresolved problems about that new cultural pattern. This has been to a large extent alluded to in Chapter Six.

For Essad and other Turkish reformers, "the Revolution" was a creation for everything, even for the place of Islam in society and thus, whether consciously or not, they gave the revolution an ultimate and religious significance. The six principles upon which the Turkish constitution is based — republicanism, nationalism, populism, e'tatism, secularism, and revolution — are taken as self-subsisting ultimates. The Islamic implications of the political ideology remain relatively unchecked. These express themselves in party claims to ultimate legitimacy and in an inability on the part of the party in power to accept the validity of an opposition, which are not in accord with flexibility appropriate in a Western principial society.

On the other hand, Islam in Turkey has not on the whole been able to redefine its own self-image and face the theological issues involved in becoming a religion primarily, in Essad's words, enthroned in man's conscience. Nor has it been able to provide a deeper religious dimension of both legitimation and judgment of the six principles which are the basis of the new cultural life. It remains, on the whole, in a conservative frame of mind in which the ideological claims are considerable, thus still posing a threat, possibly a great one, to return the society to a less differential level of social organization. Considering the trends of the last twenty years, however, we seem to be observing a differentiation in the process of becoming, but it is not too soon to say that it has been entirely accomplished.

Other examples of the process of shifting from a prescriptive type to a principial type are numerous. For instance, communism is an example of secular political ideology which successfully came to power in the prescriptive, religiously based societies of Russia and China. But communism itself makes an ultimate religious and ideological claim, and here, as in the case of Turkey, a secular ideology claiming religious ultimacy has embarked on courses of action which hinder, rather than further, the transition to the technicist, modern principial society. It is perhaps safe to say that alongside the serious political and economic problems which communism faces today is the perhaps even more serious cultural problem—the problem of differentiation of religious and ideological levels.

In concluding this chapter, it seems worth while to stress that the processes of secularization in Islamic societies, which is, in part, what the transition from prescriptive to principial society is, does not mean that Islam as a religion disappears, as demonstrated in Chapter Six. The function of religion in a principial society is different from that in a prescriptive society, but it is not necessarily less important. Moreover, in the very process of transition, Islam may reappear in many new guises. Perhaps, what makes the situation so unclear is its very fluidity. Even in highly differentiated societies of the West, such as the United States, traditional Christianity so deeply associated with the prescriptive past, is still in the process of finding its place in modern, technologically advanced American principial society. Nevertheless, what is proposed here is a feasible alternative at the present time; the stark reality is that xenophobic nationalism is gaining ground because of, and at the expense of, Islam, in the larger part of the Muslim world. If this trend continues, Islam will have to do some basic re-thinking of its position to survive at all.

PROBLEMS AND PROSPECTS

CHAPTER TEN

PROBLEMS AND PROSPECTS

Events in the Muslim world seem to repeat the past. The newspapers are filled with sudden deaths of Muslim regimes and alliances, with tales of rivalries and rebellions. Yet the issues and the context in which they are fought are entirely new. The modern age has brought about a dying more important than the death of kings; it has also introduced a greater chance to be creative and a greater need to make choices than has confronted any previous generation of Muslims. The stakes are greater, too, because there are more Muslims alive today than in any time in Islam's preceding history.

Today's Muslim revolution is not merely a revolution of rulers or rising expectations. The cumulative growth of ideas, production, and power generated outside the Islamic system has penetrated that system and is tearing apart its repetitive pattern of balanced tension. A system connecting man, God, and society is falling apart and the new forces are still too far out of balance, sometimes even out of touch, with the old and with each other to constitute a stable and resilient new pattern. Many vital elements of Islam are likely to persist for centuries to come, but they will need to be related to each other in new ways. The traditional system of which they once formed a part cannot be recovered, for important segments are already missing (e.g. the diminishing role of ulema), and the rest have therefore lost their essential links, and their relevance in the contemporary world and therefore their effectiveness.

The head of the Islamic community, the caliph, no longer exists. Protests from other Muslim communities did not deter the Turks in 1924 from abolishing his office (Berkes 1964). Conferences among Muslims in Cairo and Mecca in 1926 and in Jerusalem in 1931 did not succeed in reviving him. The caliphate has ceased to be even an issue in the rising decay of Muslim national cultures.

The Islamic empire is also dead. The demise of its last incarnation, the Ottoman Empire, is mourned neither by Turks nor by Arabs. No Islamic bloc of nations has since emerged, nor are there any significant forces now working in that direction. The Islamic World Congress, a non-governmental body founded in Karachi, Pakistan, in 1949, has suffered from lack of effectiveness since the very beginning as a result of the patent efforts, first of Pakistan and later of Egypt, to control its operations and policies for national ends, and for a time from its exploitation by the neo-Islamic totalitarian groups for prestige and funds. A similar congress organized by Saudi Arabia in May, 1962, which instituted an Islamic League, was intended primarily to counter Egyptian and socialist influences in the Islamic world. Pan Islam, a mere specter when Sultan Abd al-Hamid of Turkey unsuccessfully invoked it during the last quarter of the nineteenth century for the political purpose of stemming secularism and disunity in his empire, no longer comprises a living community.

The ulema are no longer the guardians of the core of the community's laws, or the only educated interpreters of its tradition, or the advisers of the ruler. The tenor of their cultural commitments, however, has not changed much with time, except in those countries where the pressure of reformist governments has been strong enough to induce the ulema to echo or sustain the new secular ideas with their own traditional voca-

bulary. Left to their own initiative, the ulema could deprive Ali
Abd al-Raziq of the certificate placing him among the ulema
because he wrote a book in 1925 suggesting that the state can and
should be separated from the religious institutions of Islam (Raziq:
1925). At the Islamic Colloquium in Lahore in winter 1957,
Syrian and other delegates demanded the withdrawal of a paper
by Muhammad Daud Rahbar, who argued that certain texts in
the Koran clearly referred to the here and now of the Prophet's
time, that these texts are no longer relevant, and by their presence
demonstrate the acceptability of further evolution of thought.
The paper was later published in the *Muslim World* (see Rahbar
1958).

Consequently, every Muslim state has established a new constitution, or a civil, criminal, or administrative code during the
past thirty years, has had it drafted by Western trained or Western
inspired lawyers rather than by the ulema. In fact, when Pakistan
—the one state formed in modern times intentionally along Islamic,
rather than cultural or historical divisions—questioned its ulema on
major issues of state and society, the inquiry became a turning
point in the country's ideological orientation. The testimony of
its leading ulema was so divided, confused, and ambiguous that
the influence of the ulema materially declined thereafter. In
Tunisia, the unwillingness of the French to abandon the medieval
theological curriculum of Zeitouna University in Tunis produced
a prolonged student strike in 1950. The protests of the ulema
against the changes, finally instituted by the independent Tunisian
government in 1958, found no response among Tunisian intellectuals
or politicians. Similarly, the efforts of the Moroccan government
to convert its ancient medieval University at Fez into a new secular
institution have elicited only token approval.

The institutions of popular Islam, the guilds and religious brotherhoods—organizations of worship, mutual help, and political
discontent—have dissolved and decayed. The economic basis of
the guilds have been undermined, for their goods could not com-
pete with the cheaper and more efficient products of modern
industry. Even the saintliness of the leaders of the religious brotherhood—traditionally assumed to be inheritable—seems to have
lost its efficacy.

In the past, many of the empires and rebellions of the Islamic realm owed their origin to the alliance of the religious brotherhood, or at least its founding saint, with a major tribe. The Almohad, Almoravid, Fatimid, and Wahabi states, among others, were formed in this way. Such a combination can still cause unrest, but it can no longer hope to seize the reins of government. No tribe can now match the technology and armaments of a central government. Coup, not conquest, is today's avenue to power. Hence, charismatic leadership, to be effective, must now resort to the machinery of urban parties and factions.

The only unit which has processed sufficient social, economic, and moral strength to survive all the past vicissitude of Islamic history—the patriarchal family and its emanations, the self-sustaining village and tribe, is ceasing to be the secure nucleus of Islamic life. With improved health measures, such a family becomes too large for the land it has traditionally occupied. With the coming of industrialization, individuals tend to go wherever jobs can be found. Kinship groups are no longer adequate in size or organization to serve as an effective unit for collective bargaining with the rest of the world (Goode 1963). They cannot overcome their present ignorance and poverty unless they participate in a larger world of new skills and markets. In many Muslim countries, the disintegration of the traditional family, with its carefully protected veiled women, is already beginning to yield among urban workers to the sustaining authority of the wage-earner mother. Goode (1963) provides illustrations such as Istanbul, Tehran, Beirut, etc.

While traditional links are shattered beyond repair, new connections are not readily available at hand. The social distance among individuals in the Muslim world is growing wider under the pressures of the modern age. The educated and the uneducated were in the past separated by the amount of knowledge they possessed about the same things. Now those who have had a modern education know something belonging to a different realm of being. Sheer physical mobility leads to the discovery that life outside the family offers choices not dreamt of in the past generation. The radio, movies, newspapers, and books allow a young person for the first time to choose his own intellectual and spiritual brothers. Modern scientific thought makes possible, indeed requires, a re-examination of all traditional relationships and structures. Whether technician, intellectual, or politician, a member of the new generation finds the traditions, skills and values of his father deficient or irrelevant. Knowledge has thus become an issue and instrument of battle.

As a result, moral and intellectual contact is broken between generations. Faced with this gap, the new generation has generally chosen to make a revolutionary leap. The Ataturks and Nassers, men in their thirties when they gained control of their country, as if age, once the one sure title to respect in the Muslim past, no longer mattered. Indeed, they act almost as if they had no ancestors.

There is also a greater gap than between the rich and the poor. In the past, 'the rich usually feared to be ostentatious lest the sultan suddenly seized their wealth. They wore, if better materials, still the same cut of clothes as the poor. They died of the same disease. Now they no longer live alike or dress alike; they need no longer die of the same disease. Today, when it has become possible for the first time in the history of human experience to alleviate and perhaps overcome poverty, the difference between rich and poor ceases to be a condition and becomes an issue in the transformation of the Muslim's cultural lot.

There has always been an important gap between city and countryside in the Muslim world. Islam was originated and elaborated in the cities, and the Koran itself, reflecting the traditional distrust between the settled and nomadic population, upbraided the bedouins for not being good Muslims. "The Arabs of the desert are keener in misbelief and hypocrisy..." (Koran IX:97). Since most of the Muslim world is still a peasant society dedicated to repeating itself in tune with the seasons, the very rhythm of its life has now become an issue. The mechanization and routinization required by modern machine and modern bureaucracy for the sake of efficiency and change demand an entirely different rhythm of life. There is a sharpening contrast between those largely urban elements now committed to production-mindedness and the discipline of the eight to ten hour day, and that largely folk majority which remains attuned to the rhythm of season. The struggle for progress and modernity thus becomes a battle between two different cultures and two different ages.

The modern age that first became visible in Western Europe between the thirteenth and fifteenth centuries and reached South-West Asia by the nineteenth and twentieth centuries is thus shattering the traditional community and structure of Islam. The new nation-states in the Muslim world are so far no more stable than their predecessors, since the new ideologies often divide kin and neighbor from each other. Escape from the revolutionary turmoil is also hindered by the lack of resources: in almost all these countries, population is growing more rapidly than production, aspirations more rapidly than accomplishments, opinions more rapidly than consensus. And there is also the great pain of starting now, so far behind other national cultures.

As early as about A.D. 1105, the great Muslim theologian al-Ghazali could write that "there is no hope in returning to a traditional faith after it has once been abandoned, since the essential condition in the holder of a traditional faith is that he should not know that he is a traditionalist. Whenever he knows that, the glass of his traditional faith is broken. That is a breaking that cannot be mended, and a separating that cannot be united by any sewing or putting together, except it be melted in the fire and given another new form" (MacDonald 1909:180). It was possible for al-Ghazali to put his faith together again by joining reason and mysticism with fear and hope in Allah. His was an inward journey at a time of intellectual doubt, spiritual corruption, and political turmoil; but it was a time that failed to give birth to a new age. Such a return seems much harder today. The existential foundations of Muslim life have been decisively altered. Those Muslims who ignored the material changes about them, or the vital spiritual and intellectual achievements of societies which do not accept Allah's final revelation to mankind, are likely to find few companions for their pilgrimage. Yet how is a modern Muslim to begin the reconstruction of his world? Reflections in this regard have been offered elsewhere in this dissertation.

Twice before the coming of the modern age, Islam successfully assimilated the concepts of other cultures without essentially changing its own character. Why not again ? In its first two centuries of existence (from about 622-820), Islam brilliantly adopted laws, customs, and institutions from cultures among which it was born as well as from those it conquered. It was relatively easy to accept ideas from societies with similar forms of social organization and value patterns and to give them an Islamic cast. During the ninth century, Islam assimilated from Hellenism scientific facts, and also ontological concepts and methods of logic for the foundation of an Islamic scholasticism, but rejected Greece's critical ideas regarding nature and justice, and the dignity of the free individual. Islam was then free to choose or not to choose. It was at the height of its zenith and power, and did not need to deal with Greece as an intellectually and economically more productive and politically more powerful society.

Islam picked only those aspects of Greek thought which would buttress its own traditional position. The majority of rulers and ulema were right to consider the remainder of Greek philosophy subversive. If Islam's Allah were no longer to be thought all-powerful, but instead lawful and just, could the all-powerful caliphs, some of whom had begun to think of themselves as deputies to Allah rather than successors to Mohammed, be less lawful and just ? If law and justice were to be thought accessible to human reason, could not both the Koran and the cailph's commands be reviewed in the light of reasonable men's judgment of what is just and lawful ? As a result of this conflict of minds in the Islamic world, Arab translations of Greek philosophy became available to help bring about the renaissance of Europe. Among the orthodox of Islam, however, the advocates of reason lost, and even those who applied it subsequently to the interpretation of dogma were fewer by far and their fate more problematical than those who applied their reason to the codification and clarification of revealed law. Orthodoxy chose not free reason but a rigidity capable of being bent only by the particular balance of tensions at any concrete moment.

The modern age, however, issues a challenge, or invitation, of quite a different order. As long as a Muslim holds that the comprehensive order revealed by Allah in the seventh century and subsequently hallowed by tradition is final and cannot be amended, he will be unable to study the world independently and scientifically in order to fashion his own world himself. The Christian breaking out of the middle ages into an era of scientific thought, could at least retain the medieval notion that God—or now the nature of nature—could to a large extent be ascertained by reason. The Muslim, by contrast, emerges from an age in which tyranny, anarchy, hunger, and death seemed often beyond remedy, an environment helping to reinforce his religious dogma that Allah was all powerful, and the moments of life were not succession of cause and effect but separate and unrelated Allah-created miracles? Only by setting his judgment against the received interpretation of life, whether through ulema, ancestors, or accustomed nature, can a Muslim now alter his history and socio-cultural environment. Only by using his individual judgment against that tradition can he escape the deepest of all Islamic inhibitions or prohibitions— that against innovation.

The reformation of Islam, however, involves far more decisive steps than reformation did in the West. It is not a matter merely of altering the relationship between the Church and State, for there is no church in Islam. No one is ordained; there is no hierarchy; each mosque is locally endowed. (The ulema are scholar-legists, not priests). Indeed, reformation cannot be confined to the realm of religion: in Allah's revelation to Mohammed, all human thought, behavior, and institutions are related to be sacred, and have meaning only in relation to it. Thus reformation in Islam means changing a total way of life, the culture and the social structure of the Muslim systems. But once that integrated pattern of values and relationships is altered, each part of it loses its original significance and meaning, it can be transmuted and integrated into a new form of life. Reformation in Islam inescapably touches not only Allah's relation to man, but also man's relation to a social system and to the values that hold it together.

Such a reformation and renaissance are well under way with varying speeds and ends. Many observers have missed this fact because their attention is drawn instead to the exceedingly few Muslims who have been at work during the past century deliberately reforming Islam to preserve its integrity as a system of faith and as a mode of behavior. It may well be that these few seek to accomplish the impossible. Can any closed system like Islam be made to mesh with an open and increasingly changing society, yet succeed in remaining a closed system ?

But if the modern Muslim must contend with an inherited system that was fixed and closed, he also received from the past an uncommonly flexible style for dealing with a world in motion. He has long known how to combine his awe for the powerful, the learned, and the successful with his more enduring respect for the consensus of the community. He can adapt resiliently to the permanent tension between justice and power, and ratify the inescapable with shrewd forebearance. Such customary flexibility has allowed the still tradition-bound masses of folk Islam to accept today's secular transformist governments, and has made it easier for the reformers to respond to the modern world with creative assimilation.

The transformation of Islam, in contrast to that of sixteenth century Christianity, is not likely to be heralded and defined through theological disputations. Rather, the change in the Islamic way of life will become visible through the reformation and rehabilitation of Muslims. This venture in cultural engineering is to some degree in progress, and the Islam that will emerge will be definable as Islam has always been defined in practice—as the pattern on interaction which relates Muslims to each other, and which, if they are fortunate, a majority among them also consider to be "good."

Such a transformed Islam, however, is bound to create a different network of social relations and cultural values than traditional Islam. Precisely for that reason, some Muslim leaders deem it prudent to call their new ways by old names, while others emphasize the thoroughness of their reforms by renouncing old symbols entirely and speaking only of socialism, nationalism, and other ideological generalizations. The road to modernization for all Muslim societies must involve a march without a final prophet, a final book, or even assurance of final success. The speed, participants, and the form of this universal Muslim fate, however, are, can, and must be shaped in each part of the Muslim world by

unique beginnings. Just as British and French ideologies or Russian
and Chinese Communism differ because of different historical
origins, so will the traditional Islamic way of life, in its transformation, help to mold the nature of modern ideologies in the Muslim
world—hence by concern for the character and depth of the
Islamic revolution.

Socio-cultural transformation, it is worth repeating, is by now
a world-wide phenomenon and therefore demands analysis that is
parochial, either Western or Islamic. This is a point that needs
especially to be made in a study of the Islamic systems, where the
problem of making new choices used to be debated as the issue of
"Westernization." Historically, that is indeed how change began.
The transformation of the Muslim world did not originate, as in
Europe, with the rise of new social classes, or the growth of new
forms of production. The metamorphosis of Islam began with the
efforts of sultans, whether in Constantinople, Cairo, Java, or
Rabat, to maintain themselves, their ideas, and the domains of
their rule intact by copying Western instruments of defense.
Westernization, once started, snowballed as Western powers took
advantage of the fact that these Muslim rulers lacked money, skill,
and strength to preserve themselves. By direct Western action,
that is by way of "imperialism," Westernization made its mark
even to the extent of supplying Muslim states with governing institutions such as constitutions and parliaments.

By now, however, the issue is no longer "Westernization" but
"modernization." It has become a native movement. The term
Westernization has itself become parochial and misleading. However much he may prefer to continue to draw upon Western
Europe, Russia and the United States for knowledge, ideas, and
assistance, the contemporary Muslim must recognize (perhaps in
contrast to his father) that being modern does not mean becoming
English, Russian, French, or American. The modern age, with its
science, technology, and cultural values, is transforming both the
Muslim and the non-Muslim impartially, and the roads to modernization that can now be chosen as models include Yugoslavia,
Japan, Italy, or China no less than the United States, Germany
or the U.S.S.R.

Westernization could not help but become a locally rooted movement. Before the modern age began, it was possible to arm, and become more prosperous and more powerful than any neighbor, without changing one's mind about anything one's ancestors held dear. Today, the price of knowledge, status, and power for the Muslim countries is conversion to an entirely new outlook. It is not feasible to buy the weapons and learn the techniques of modern warfare, and yet preserve ancient traditions. The Ottoman had the illusion that it is. The new Turks knew that they had to abandon it, as carefully articulated by Ataturk in a speech in 1925: "Before the impetuous torrent of civilization, resistance is futile, it is quite without mercy towards the heedless and refractory. In the face of the might and superiority of civilization, which pierces mountains, flies in the sky, sees everything from the atom invisible to the eye to the stars, and which enlightens and investigates, nations striving to advance with a medieval mentality and primitive superstitions are condemned to perish or at least to be enslaved and humiliated. But the people of the Turkish republic have decided to live to eternity as a civilized and progressive community, and have torn to pieces the chains of slavery with a heroism unequaled in history" (Berkes 1964).

Social change in the Muslim world has taken place unevenly and remains incomplete. Here the modern age has deprived more men of customary satisfaction, and denied more men the fulfillment of their newly raised expectations, than it has so far expanded opportunities for a meaningful, productive and a richer life. It has served to undermine old institutions more decisively than it has yet initiated the effective development of new ones. Almost everywhere, cultural transformation has outrun institutional reforms.

To effectuate a new and effective socio-cultural design in the Muslim world means above all to overcome these imbalances. It means fashioning a social structure that can accommodate newly emerging social classes, new values, and new relationships among individuals. It means forming institutions resilient enough to overcome the present crisis of uncontrolled change, and capable of transforming further change into evolutionary, stabilizing, cultural development.

Concern with the roots of social relationships and structural components of the Muslim systems has thus become the test for the relevance and survival of Islam and its subscribers. Whether to create such new roots, who is to deal with them, what price to pay for the effort, and who and what is to pay for it—these have now become the principal issues which require much thinking, research, soul-searching and compromise. The principal model proposed in the previous chapter provides only the broadest framework for such an undertaking. Nevertheless, it is my hope that what I have proposed theoretically, will provide the foundation and stimulation for action and theoretical and applied *concern* (rather than interest) on the part of anthropologists and other social scientists.

One final note might be added. Although certain religious conservatives and secular extremists continue to blame the West (and recently the East) for the fact that they must face this issue now, before the caravan of human achievements is too far ahead to catch; the fight is no longer between the modern West and the medieval variety of Islam, or between the local technicists and the traditional folk Muslim masses. The conflict now takes place among and within the Muslim systems themselves, and until they have dealt with the roots of their problems, change in the Muslim sphere will continue to be frequent, haphazard, sudden, discontinuous, and violent. Islam must be transformed before its cancerous traditional aspects disable and obliterate that which is still healthy and reparable.

BIBLIOGRAPHY

BIBLIOGRAPHY

ABBOTT, FREELAND
 1968 *Islam and Pakistan.* Ithaca: Cornell University Press.

ABDALLAH, ABD AL-AZIZ BEN
 1951 "Islam and Communism," *Al-Alam* (Arabic newspaper). Rabat,
  Morocco. June 27, 1951.

ADAMS, CHARLES C.
 1933 *Islam and Modernism in Egypt.* London : Oxford University Press.

ALLEN, HENRY E.
 1935 *The Turkish Transformation.* Chicago : The University of Chicago
  Press.

ALMOND, G., and JAMES C. COLEMAN (eds)
 1960 *The Politics of Developing Areas.* Princeton: Princeton University
  Press.

AMIN, OSMAN
 1957 "The Modernist Movement in Egypt," Richard N. Frey, *Islam and
  The West.* The Hague : Mouton.

ANDERSON, ARNOLD D., and MARY JEAN BOWEN (eds)
 1965 *Education and Economic Development.* Chicago: Aldine.

AYAL, ELIEZER B.
 1966 "National Ideology and Economic Development," *Human Organization,*
  Vol. 25, No. 3, pp. 230-239.

ANSHEN, RUTH NANDA (ed)
1959 *The Family*. New York: Harper and Rowe.

BAER, GABRAEL
1964 *Population and Society in the Arab East*. London : Routledge and Kegan Paul.

BANTON, MICHAEL (ed)
1966 *The Social Anthropology of Complex Societies*. Edinburgh: Tavistock Publications.

BARNETT, H. G.
1953 *Innovation: The Basis of Cultural Change*. New York: McGraw-Hill.

BECKER, HOWARD
1957 "Current Sacred-Secular Theory and Its Development," Howard Becker and Alvin Boskoff (eds), *Modern Sociological Theory in Continuity and Change*. New York: Dryden Press.

BERGER, MORROE
1962 *The Arab World Today*. New York : Doubleday and Company.

BERKES, NIYAZI
1964 *The Development of Secularism in Turkey*. Montreal: McGill University Press.

BOURDEAU, PIERRE
1962 *The Algerians*. Boston: Beacon Press.

BROCKELMANN, CARL
1960 *History of the Islamic People*. New York: Capricorn Press.

CHAMBERS, RICHARD II
1964 "The Civil Bureaucracy: Turkey," Robert E. Ward and Dunkwart A. Rustow (eds). Princeton: Princeton University Press.

COLEMAN, JAMES S.
1965 *Education and Political Development*. Princeton: Princeton University Press.

COULSON, NOEL J.
1964 *A History of Islamic Law*. Edinburgh: Edinburgh University Press.

CRAGG, KENNETH
1955 "The Modernist Movement in Egypt," H.A.R. Gibb and Harold Bowen, *Islamic Society and The West*. London: Oxford University Press.

DAGHESTANI, KAZEM
1953 "Evolution of The Muslim Family in the Middle Eastern Countries," UNESCO : *International Social Science Bulletin*, Vol. 5, No. 4.

DESANTILLANA, DAVID
1931 "Law and Society," Sir Thomas Arnold and Alfred Guillaume, *The Legacy of Islam*. London: Clarendon Press.

DUNCAN, B. MACDONALD
1909 *The Religious Attitude and Life in Islam*. Chicago : The University of Chicago Press.

EISENSDADT, S.N.
1966 *Modernization: Protest and Change*. Englewood Cliffs: Prentice-Hall.

FISHER, SYDNEY N.
  1959 *The Middle East : A History.* New York : Doubleday and Company.
FREY, FREDERICK W.
  1964 "Turkey," Robert E. Ward and Dankwart Rustow (eds), *Political Modernization in Japan and Turkey.* Princeton: Princeton University Press.
  1965 *The Turkish Political Elite.* Cambridge: The M.I.T. Press.
GAUDFROY-DEMOMBYNES, MAURICE
  1954 *Muslim Institutions.* London: Allen and Unwin.
GEERTZ, CLIFFORD
  1960 *The Religion of Java.* New York: The Free Press.
  1968 *Islam Observed: Religious Developments in Morocco and Indonesia.* New Haven: Yale University Press.
GHAZALLI, ABU HAMID AL
  1953 *The Faith and Practice of al-Gazalli.* Translation of Ghazalli's works by W. Montgomery Watt. London: Oxford University Press.
GIBB, H.A.R.
  1947 *Modern Trends in Islam.* Chicago: The University of Chicago Press.
GOODE, WILLIAM J.
  1963 *World Revolution and Family Patterns.* New York : The Free Press.
GILLESPIE, JAMES M., and GORDON ALLPORT
  1955 *Youth's Outlook on the Future: A cross-national study.* Garden City: Doubleday and Company.
HAGEN, E.E.
  1962a "A Framework for Analyzing Economic and Political Change," Robert Asher, *Development and Emerging Countries: An Agenda For Research.* Washington, D.C., Brookings Institute.
  1962b *On the Theory of Social Change.* Homewood: The Dorsey Press
HARRIS, GEORGE L. (ed)
  1958 *Iraq.* New Haven: HRAF.
HIMADEH, SAID B.
  1951 "Economic Factors Underlying Social Problems in the Middle East." *Middle East.* Vol. 5. Summer 1951.
HITTI, PHILIP
  1962 "Islam and The Modern World," in *Studies on Asia,* edited by Sydney D. Brown. Lincon : University of Nebraska Press.
HOEBEL, E. ADAMSON
  1964 *The Law of Primitive Man.* Cambridge : Harvard University Press.
  1965 "Fundamental Cultural Postulates and Judicial Law Making in Pakistan," AA 67:43-56.
HOURANI, A.H.
  1947 *Minorities in the Arab World.* New York : Oxford University Press.
HOROWITZ, IRVING L.
  1964 "Sociological and Ideological Conception of Industrial Development," *American Journal of Economics and Sociology,* No. 23.

HOSELITZ, BERT F.
1963 "Main Concepts in the Analysis of the Social Implications of Tecnological Change," Bert F. Hoselitz and Wilbert Moore (eds), *Industrialization and Society*. The Hague: Mouton.

HUDSON, C. F.
1952 "Why Asians Hate the West," *Commentary*, Vol. 13, May 1952.

HYMAN, HERBERT H. and ARIF PAYASLIOGLO and FREDERICK FREY
1958 "The Values of Turkish College Youth," *Public Opinion Quarterly*, Vol. 22, No. 3.

IQBAL, MOHAMMED
1934 *The Reconstruction of Religious Thought in Islam*. London : Oxford University Press.

JACOBS, NORMAN
1967 *The Sociology of Development: Iran as an Asian Case Study*. New York: Frederick A. Praeger.

JEFFERY, ARTHUR
1942 "The Political Importance of Islam," *Journal of Near Eastern Studies*, Vol. 1.

KARPAT, KEMAL H.
1959 *Turkey's Politics: The Transition to a Multiparty System*. Princeton: Princeton University Press.

KERR, MALCOLM H.
1966 *Islamic Reform*. Berkeley: The University of California Press.

KHADDURI, MAJID
1955 *War and Peace in the Law of Islam*. Baltimore: Johns Hopkins University Press.
1956 "From Religious to National Law," Ruth Nanda Anshen (ed), *Mid-East: World Center*. New York : Harper and Brothers.
1959 "The Islamic System : Its Competition and Coexistence With Western Systems," *Proceedings of the American Society of International Law*.

KHADDURI, MAJID and HERBERT J. LIEBESNY (eds)
1955 *Law in the Middle East*, Vol. I: "Origins and Development of Islamic Law." Washington : Middle East Institute.

KHALDUN, IBN
1958 *The Muqaddemah: An Introduction to History* (3 Volumes). Translated by Franz Rosenthal. New York : Bollingen.

KHALID, MOHAMMED KHALID
1953 *From Here We Start*. American Council of Learned Societies. Washington, D.C., Near Eastern Translation Program. No. 3.

KISSLING, HANS JOACHIM
1954 "The Sociological and Educational Role of the Dervish Orders in the Ottoman Empire," Gustav E. von Grunebaum (ed), *Studies in Islamic Cultural History*. AA 56, No. 2, part 2.

KORAN, THE
1949 *Koran*. (Translated by E. H. Palmer). London : Oxford University Press.

KRITZECK, JAMES
1959 "Portrait of Ahmad: A report on a typical member of Egypt's rising new middle class," *Commonwealth*, December 11.

LASSWELL, HAROLD D. and ABRAHAM KAPLAN
1950 *Power and Society*. New Haven: Yale University Press.

LASSWELL, HAROLD D., *et al.*
1952 *The Comparative Study of Elites*. Hooever Institute Studies, Series B. No. 1. Stanford : Stanford University Press.

LERNER, DANIEL
1964 *The Passing of Traditional Society: Modernizing the Middle East*. Glencoe : The Free Press.

LEVINE, ROBERT A.
1966 *Dreams and Deeds: Achievement Motivation in Nigeria*. Chicago: University of Chicago Press.

LEVY, MARION J. JR.
1966 *Modernization and the Structure of Society*. Princeton: Princeton University Press.

LEVY, REUBEN
1957 *The Social Structure of Islam*. Cambridge: Cambridge University Press.

LEWIS, BERNARD
1937 "The Islamic Guilds," *Economic Review*, November 1937.

LEWIS, BERNARD
1940a "Some observations on the significance of heresy in the history of Islam," *Studia Islamica*, Vol. 1.
1940b *The Origins of Ismailism*. Cambridge: Cambridge University Press.
1961 *The Emergence of Modern Turkey*. London: Oxford University Press.

MACDONALD, DUNCAN B.
1909 *The Religious Attitude and Life In Islam*. Chicago: The University of Chicago Press.

MAKAL, MAHMUD
1954 *A Village in Anatolia*. London: Valentine Mitchel and Company.

MANHEIM, KARL
1940 *Man and Society in an Age of Reconstruction*. London: Kegan Paul.

MAYNARD, RICHARD
1961 *The Lise and its Curriculum in the Turkish Educational System*. Ph.D. dissertion. The University of Chicago.

McCLELLAND, DAVID
1961 *The Achieving Society*. New York: D. Van Nostrand Company.
1963 "National Character and Economic Growth in Turkey and Iran," Lucian Pye (ed), *Communication and Political Development*. Princeton: Princeton University Press.

MEAD, MARGARET
1956 *New Lives for Old: Cultural Transformation—Manus 1928-1953*. New York.

MOORE, WILBERT E.
1965 *The Impact of Industry.* Englewood Cliffs: Prentice-Hall.
NERMIN, ERDENTUG
1959 *A Study of the Social Structure of a Turkish Village.* Ankara : Ayyildiz Matbaasi.
NEW YORK TIMES
1959 September 7, "Arab Unit Warns West of Algeria," p. 3
1960 November 11, "Secularist Protest," p. 14
NIVISON, DAVID and ARTHUR F. WRIGHT (eds)
1959 *Confusianism in Action.* Stanford: Stanford University Press.
NOLTE, RICHARD H.
1958 "The Rule of Law in the Arab Middle East," *The Muslim World,* October 1958.
PIERCE, JOE
1964 *Life in a Turkish Village.* New York: Holt, Rinehart and Winston.
RAHBAR, MOHAMMAD DAUD
1958 "The Challenge of Modern Ideas and Social Values to Muslim Society," *The Muslim World,* October 1958.
RAHMAN, FAZLUR
1966 *Islam.* New York : Holt, Rinehart and Winston.
ROSENTHAL, ERWIN I. J.
1958 *Political Thought in Medieval Islam.* Cambridge: Cambridge University Press.
RAZIQ ALI ABD AL-
1925 *al-Islam Wa Usul al Hukum* (Islam and the Fundamentals of Authority). Cairo. n.p.
RIESMAN, DAVID
1954 *Individualism Reconsidered.* New York: The Free Press.
ROBINSON, RICHARD D.
1950 "An Analysis of Turkish Education," Paper prepared for the International Bank of Reconstruction, International Bank of Reconstruction Economic Survey Series.
1963 *The First Turkish Republic.* Cambridge: Harvard University Press.
SCHACHT, JOSEPH
1950 *The Origins of Mohammaden Jurisprudence.* London: Oxford University Press.
1964 *Introduction to Islamic Law.* London: Oxford University Press.
SMITH, WILFRED CANTWELL
1946 *Modern Islam in India.* London: Oxford University Press.
1955 "The Intellectuals in the Modern Development of the Islamic World," Sidney N. Fisher, *Social Forces in the Middle East.* Ithaca : Cornell University Press.

1966 *Islam in Modern History.* Princeton, Princeton University Press.
SMITH, W. ROBERTSON
1903 *Kinship and Marriage in Early Arabia.* Boston: Beacon Press.
STIRLING, PAUL
1953 "Social Ranking in a Turkish Village," *British Journal of Sociology.* 4:31-44.
1965 *Turkish Village.* New York: Wiley.
SWEETMAN, J. W.
1957 "View Point in Pakistan I," *The Muslim World,* June.
THOMAS, LEWIS V. and RICHARD N. FREY
1952 *The United States and Turkey and Iran.* Cambridge: Harvard University Press.
TOYNBEE, ARNOLD
1954 *A Study of History,* Vol. VIII. London: Oxford University Press.
VEXLIARD, ALEXANDER, and KEMAL AYATACH
1964 "The Village Institutes in Turkey," *Comparative Education Review,* Vol. VIII, No. 1.
VON GRUNEBAUM, GUSTAV E.
1954 *Studies in Islamic Cultural History.* AA 56, No. 2, part 2.
1955 *Islam, Essays in the Nature and Growth of a Cultural Tradition.* AA 27, No. 2, memoir No. 81.
——, (ed)
1955 *Unity and Diversity in Muslim Civilization.* Chicago: University of Chicago Press.
WATT, W. MONTGOMERY
1961 *Islam and the Integration of Society.* Evanston: Northwestern University Press.
WARD, ROBERT E. and DANKWART A. RUSTOW (eds)
1964 *Political Modernization in Japan and Turkey.* Princeton: Princeton University Press.
WILSON, GODREY and MONICA WILSON
1945 *The Analysis of Social Change.* Cambridge: Cambridge University Press.
YASA, IBRAHIM
1957 *Hasanolan: Socio-Economic Structure of a Turkish Village.* Ankara: Yeni Matbaa.
ZURYAK, COSTI K.
1949 "The Essence of Arab Civilization," *The Middle East Journal,* Vol. 3, April 1949.

INDEX

INDEX